Any Which Way But Meat

To Dad, Susan, Jules + Alan,

It was great to see you again!
I love you a lot and hope
to see you a lot more often.
Love Tracy Montero

Julie Lilly and Tracy Montero

Illustrations by Mike Falco

Library of Congress Cataloging-in-Publication Data

Lilly, Julie, 1960-
    Any which way but meat.

    1. Vegetarian cookery. I. Montero, Tracy, 1960-   . II. Title
TX837.L48 1989   641.5'636   89-13350

ISBN 0-927444-02-X

Published by
Lilly & Belote Publishers
P.O. Box 57414, Sherman Oaks, CA 91413

Typesetting and page layout by **Word Wizards®**
Sherman Oaks, CA

Printed in the United States of America
by Griffin Printing, Glendale, CA

I do feel that spiritual progress does demand at some stage that we should cease to kill our fellow creatures for the satisfaction of our bodily wants.

— Gandhi

I have no doubt that it is a part of the destiny of the human race, in its gradual improvement, to leave off eating animals.

— Thoreau

Dedication

To Bill, George, Lanny, Tasha and Nadeen,
for giving their hearts, minds, souls and
taste buds to this project

and to Claire and Ross who give
the confidence to do anything

TABLE OF CONTENTS

Page

Any Which Way But Meat

Acknowledgements

From Tracy:

Special thanks to Esther and Emil Montero for their wisdom shared in gardening, the use of home-grown vegetables, and the traditional combined tastes from the East and West. And to Lanny for all of his help, support and suggestions in the kitchen, and over the writing tablets and computer.

From Julie:

What we are can depend greatly on what our parents were. I would like to thank my mother, Joan, for her great independence and strength, and for having the courage to say, "I don't know" if she didn't.

I would also like to thank my father, Ross Hagen, and my stepmother, Claire. No words could ever say enough for what they have done for me. They are two very strong lights in this world, who insist on seeing only the best in others. They have taught me that nothing is impossible.

I would like to especially thank my husband, Bill, for all his support. I don't think there is anything that the two of us couldn't do. His examples of gentleness, open-mindedness and infinite patience have added priceless pearls to our relationship, and to me as a person.

To Tracy Montero for her input and half the recipes in this book. Thanks for making the trek to California, sweating in the kitchen with me, and typing 'til we dropped. A friendship that survived this can survive anything!

To Bob, Jill, Alex, Lisa, Ray and Gray — because I love you.

To Doug Dunn at Word Wizards — his constant creative help, support, friendship and business knowledge have helped open the way to the top.

And to Mike Falco for his God-given sense of humor, his childlike outlook on life which so many of us lose, and for complimenting this book with his artwork.

All thanks to God—all ideas are gifts from Him.

Foreword

by
William Belote

My goal in writing this foreword is to share my enthusiasm for our new, meatless diet. My excitement is that of the new convert. I haven't the desire or qualifications to preach to anyone, or to lay a guilt trip on people. My own conversion to a meatless diet is only a few years old and I wasn't a "bad" person then and a "good" person now. Furthermore, I am not an expert on nutrition. Unfortunately, there is so much conflicting information on the subject that it is hard to know who to believe. If we simply compare our digestive tracts and teeth with other animals, it is clear that we resemble the fruit and vegetable eaters, not the meat eaters.

Let me give you something to think about—something basic to your common senses:

Suppose you were walking through beautiful, rolling hills of trees and grass. Then, suppose you came upon the day-old carcass of a cow. What is your reaction, your gut feeling? Are you hungry? A true meat-eater would be licking his chops and thanking his lucky stars for the good fortune of finding this "real food". A true meat eater likes to eat its meat raw, and loves to eat the guts raw, too. The fact that this doesn't sound pleasant to us should be a clue as to our natural tendencies. In order for us to find meat attractive, it must be slaughtered for us, butchered, often color-dyed, cooked, spiced and sometimes even given a nice name like "veal" so the menu doesn't read "Dead-Calf Cutlets".

It doesn't matter how many celebrities get on TV and talk about beef as "real food". If you stand next to a cow or steer, you may want to talk to it or pet it, but not kill it and eat it. Real food is an orange you can pick, peel and eat right off the tree, a carrot you can pull from the ground, grains that can be made into bread.

My own experience is that I haven't missed having meat at all. Instead of feeling like there is a hole in my diet, I am amazed at the abundance of foods and fun new ways of eating. Going meatless hasn't meant deprivation, but rather the freedom to try new things and to eat old standards like spaghetti or sloppy joe's in new ways.

I know that making changes in our basic activities like eating meat can be difficult, even scary. I can assure you that the recipes Julie Lilly and Tracy Montero have come up with will satisfy your taste buds. This book is hardly some saintly prescription to eat a simple, bland diet, though more power to you should that be your route. This is a cookbook for people who love to eat fun, spicy foods. You may realize that it wasn't the hamburger you loved, it was the steak sauce, lettuce, onion, pickle, mayo, mustard, cheese on a toasted bun. There are no limits.

May you, too, enjoy eating *Any Which Way But Meat!*

Introduction

by
Julie Lilly

My husband and I always knew that one day we would take the "leap" into becoming Vegetarians. We grew to feel hypocritical about eating animals that came nicely packaged from the store when we were unwilling to do the butchering ourselves.

Well, we made our New Year's resolution and I bravely set out in the kitchen with the fruits and vegetables, wondering how many ways I could make a carrot interesting. What followed, I might safely say these days, was like a cosmic blast. The ideas and inspirations came flowing in by the dozens! We couldn't believe the variety of meals and flavors coming out of the kitchen, as opposed to the typical tuna or turkey sandwich. Now we can honestly say that we've never enjoyed eating more in our lives.

Then came the test of eating this new way with family and friends. I didn't want to say, "We're vegetarians now," because I hate labels, and everyone always looks at you like you're weird until they accept the idea. We do a fair amount of entertaining. "Will our family and non-vegetarian friends be able to enjoy this food?" I asked myself. Thank God we were brave and tried. It's almost embarrassing, hearing the rave reviews over our dinner table, with people always asking for recipes. "Maybe I'll write a cookbook someday," I thought to myself. "Nah, I'm a full-time photographer, and too career-minded. It's not for me," I concluded.

Then, along came Tracy, my best friend in High School, who I hadn't seen in ten years. She called, and our friendship was immediately back in full force. While visiting us, she prepared some of the most delicious vegetarian meals we've had, which later led us to many phone conversations centered around new recipes. "Maybe *we* should write a cookbook," I asked her. *"Any Which Way But Meat."* **"Yes!"** we both said loudly at the same time. So for months we did nothing but cook and experiment, while fattening up our family and friends. This book is full of the top results that we would like to share with you.

Enjoy

Some of the recipes in this book include dairy products. Future editions of the book may provide alternative options with recommended substitutions, or without dairy products altogether.

Many of the recipes in this book call for "mayonnaise" or "butter". These terms are used in a generic sense; those who wish to avoid animal fats completely may wish to substitute Miracle Whip (or any no-cholesterol alternative) for mayonnaise, and margarine in place of butter.

Appetizers and Snacks

The Disappearing Dip

We couldn't ask for a more appropriate title than this one. Your guests will try to leave the platter alone after a bite or two, but the taste will simply possess them, and they'll wander back for more, and more, until...it disappears.

4-5	medium avocados, ripe
1/4 cup + 3 tbsp	mayonnaise
1 1/4 cups + 3 tbsp	sour cream
1 tbsp	Pickapeppa sauce
1/2 tsp	salt
1/2 tsp	pepper
1/2 tsp	Vege-Sal All Purpose Seasoning
1/4 tsp	cayenne pepper
1/4 tsp	hot pepper sauce
2.5 oz	package Lawry's Taco Seasoning Mix
1	large red onion, diced
4	medium size tomatoes, chopped
8-10 oz	sharp cheddar cheese, grated
1-2	bags tortilla chips

In a medium-sized mixing bowl, add avocados, 3 table-spoons mayonnaise, 3 tablespoons sour cream, Pickapeppa sauce, salt, pepper, Vege-Sal Seasoning, cayenne pepper, and hot pepper sauce. Mix with an electric mixer on medium speed until smooth; spread evenly over a 14 inch serving platter.

In another mixing bowl, stir together 1 1/4 cups sour cream, 1/4 cup mayonnaise, and the Taco Seasoning Mix until well combined; spread evenly on top of the avocado layer.

Next, evenly sprinkle on the onions and tomatoes, followed by the grated cheese.

Serve with 1-2 bags of tortilla chips, and enjoy the rave reviews.

Artichoke Parmesan Dip

12 oz	jar marinated artichoke hearts
5 oz	fresh Parmesan cheese, grated (approx. 1½ cups)
1¼ cups	mayonnaise

In a mixing bowl, beat cheese and mayonnaise until well blended. Strain juice from artichoke hearts and chop. Stir into cheese mixture.

Bake in a 425° oven in a glass oven-proof dish for 20 minutes or until dip is heated thoroughly, but not separated. Lay a paper towel over top of dip to remove any excess oil that comes to the surface. Serve hot with your favorite crackers for dipping. Makes 8-10 servings.

Baked Taco Dip

16 oz.	can vegetarian refried beans
2/3 cup	enchilada sauce
7 oz	can diced green chilies
1 cup	grated sharp cheddar cheese, firmly packed
8 oz	sour cream
1	package taco seasoning mix
3.8 oz	can sliced ripe olives
1/2 cup	onions, diced
1/2 cup	tomatoes, diced
2/3 cup	lettuce, shredded

In a bowl, combine beans, enchilada sauce, green chilies and cheese. In a 425° oven, bake bean mixture for 20 minutes in a 8x8x2 inch baking pan.

Stir together the sour cream and taco seasoning mix. Pour over top of hot bean mixture, spreading evenly.

Alternately place olives, onions and tomatoes in rows covering the entire top. Around the outer edge sprinkle lettuce. Serve warm with tortilla chips. Makes 12-15 servings.

Cannonball Dip

2	big bunches fresh spinach, rinsed and trimmed
16 oz	sour cream (1 lb.)
1 cup	mayonnaise
1.4 oz	package dry leek soup mix, or vegetable soup mix (vegetarian)
2	bunches scallions, finely chopped
8 oz	can sliced water chestnuts, chopped
1	bunch radishes, finely chopped
1 lb	loaf round sourdough bread

Put spinach and $1/2$ cup water in a large saucepan over high heat until water begins to boil. Reduce heat to low, cover, and continue steaming approx. 2 minutes, or until spinach is just wilted. Do not over cook. Drain, then let cool. Squeeze spinach as dry as possible, then finely chop.

Stir together the sour cream, mayonnaise, soup mix, onions, water chestnuts, radishes, and spinach until well blended.

Slice a lid from the top of the bread. Hollow inside of bread and tear into bite-size pieces for dipping. Spoon the spinach mixture into the hollowed out loaf. Chill. Cut up cold vegetables are also great with this dip. Makes 15-20 servings.

The Olive and Cheese Act

¹/₂ cup	butter (softened)
2 cups	firmly packed grated sharp cheddar cheese (approx. 10 oz.)
1 cup	flour
¹/₄ tsp	paprika
¹/₂ tsp	salt
1 tbsp	milk
6.7 oz	jar pimento stuffed green olives

Drain liquid from olives and place on a plate lined with paper towel. Pat olives dry.

In a large mixing bowl, whip butter until fluffy. Add cheese and mix well until cheese blends with butter. Sift into cheese mixture the flour, paprika and salt, and blend alternately with the milk until well blended. If the dough becomes too hard to handle with the beaters, switch to a wooden spoon. Cover bowl with plastic wrap and refrigerate 30 minutes or until cheese mixture is firm enough to handle.

Take approximately 1 teaspoon of cheese mixture and place olive in the middle. Roll in the palm of your hand until completely covered. Drop the olives on an ungreased cookie sheet and bake at 425° for approx 12 min. or until lightly browned. Transfer cooked olives onto a wire rack and let cool. Serve warm or at room temperature. Makes approximately 8 dozen.

Not So Deviled Eggs

12	eggs, hard boiled
¹/₄ cup	mayonnaise
1 tbsp	Dijon mustard
¹/₄ tsp	Vege-Sal All Purpose Seasoning
2	scallions, finely chopped
1	large mushroom, finely chopped
¹/₂ tsp	salt
¹/₄ tsp	pepper

Shell eggs and slice in half lengthwise. Gently remove the yolks into a mixing bowl. Add mayonnaise, mustard, Vege-Sal All Purpose Seasoning, scallions, mushroom, salt and pepper. Mix with electric mixer on low speed, scrapping the sides of the bowl with a wooden spoon until creamy. Add one heaping teaspoon of the mixture into each of the egg white halves, and arrange on a serving tray. Cover eggs and refrigerate until ready to serve. (Leftover filling or eggs can be used as egg salad in a sandwich!) Makes 24 halves.

Double Stuffed Mushrooms

12	extra large mushrooms, scrubbed well. Remove caps from stems and set aside.
1¹/₂ tbsp	olive oil

Stuffing number one:

1	slice whole wheat bread
2 tbsp	butter
4	garlic cloves, pressed
6	mushroom stems, chopped finely
¹/₂ tsp	salt
¹/₄ tsp	garlic salt
¹/₂ tsp	pepper
2¹/₂ oz	Parmesan cheese, grated

Stuffing number two:

2 tbsp	butter
¹/₄ cup	zucchini, chopped
6	mushroom stems, chopped finely
2	scallions, chopped finely
¹/₂ cup	cheddar cheese, grated
¹/₃ tsp	Vege-Sal All Purpose Seasoning

To make stuffing number one: tear bread slice into pieces, and blend in the blender for a few seconds to create fresh bread crumbs.

Melt butter in a small skillet. Add bread crumbs, garlic, mushroom stems, salt, garlic salt, pepper, and Parmesan cheese. Gently stir over medium low heat until cheese melts. Set aside.

To make stuffing number two: melt butter in a small skillet. Add mentioned ingredients and stir over low heat until cheese melts.

Stuff 6 mushroom caps with stuffing number one, and the remaining 6 mushroom caps with stuffing number two.

Place all stuffed mushrooms on a baking pan and brush tops with $1^1/_2$ tablespoons olive oil. Bake in a 350° oven for 5-7 minutes until heated through. Serve immediately. Makes 12 stuffed mushrooms.

Bean-less Nachos

Most Nacho recipes call for beans, which is fine if used as a main course. We take the beans out for this appetizer so, your guests will have room for the entrée. As it turns out, you don't even miss them.

6 oz	tortilla chips
³/₄ cup	Jack cheese, grated
³/₄ cup	cheddar cheese, grated
2	medium size tomatoes, chopped
6	scallions, chopped
¹/₃ cup	ripe olives, sliced
1	large ripe avocado
¹/₂ cup +	
1 tbsp	sour cream
1 tbsp	mayonnaise
¹/₄ tsp	salt
¹/₄ tsp	pepper
¹/₄ tsp	cayenne pepper
¹/₄ tsp	Vege-Sal All Purpose Seasoning
1 tsp	Pickapeppa sauce

Assemble chips on medium sized oven proof platter. Evenly sprinkle both grated cheeses on top of the chips. Next, evenly layer in order the tomatoes, scallions, and olives. Bake in a 350° oven for 5-10 minutes, or until cheese is melted. While nachos are baking, make avocado mixture.

In a small bowl, add the avocado, 1 tbsp sour cream, mayonnaise, salt, pepper, cayenne, Vege-Sal All Purpose Seasoning, and Pickapeppa sauce. Mix well with a fork.

When you remove nachos from oven, scoop $^1/_2$ cup sour cream in the middle with two scoops avocado mixture on each side. Serve immediately.

Great Guacamole

4	small or 2 large ripe avocados
1	med. sized lime, juiced
2	garlic cloves, minced
$^1/_4$ tsp	pesto paste (see recipe page 20)
1 tsp	Pickapeppa sauce
$^1/_8$ tsp	cayenne pepper
$^1/_4$ tsp	salt (or to taste)
$^1/_4$ cup	chopped onions
1	med. sized tomato diced

Mash avocados with a potato masher or fork, until they are easy to work with. Stir in the lime juice, garlic, pesto paste, Pickapeppa sauce, cayenne pepper, and salt. Stir well until avocado mixture is the desired texture. (We like ours chunky.) Add in the chopped onions and tomatoes, serve with tortilla chips. Makes 2 cups.

Fresh Salsa

5	medium tomatoes, chopped fine (liquid drained)
1	medium onion, chopped fine
²/₃ cup	cilantro
1	fresh lemon, juiced
1	small fresh jalapeño pepper
1 tsp	salt

Put 1 cup chopped tomatoes and all of the onions in a medium sized bowl. Set aside.

Add the remaining tomatoes, cilantro, lemon juice, jalapeño pepper, and salt into a blender. Blend until well combined. Pour mixture into the bowl of chopped tomatoes and onions; stir well and serve.

Additional suggested uses:
- Serve with guacamole.
- Serve on the side with nachos and other Mexican dishes.
- Great on top of omelettes.
- Nice addition to salads and sandwiches.

Salads and Dressings

Pesto Paste

Several recipes in this book will call for pesto paste. Pesto paste is a very concentrated blend of herbs and oil. We have found it to have a very versatile taste that blends well with vegetables, salad dressings, sauces, pastas, etc. This recipe is made extra large so you will have plenty of paste when needed. The additional paste stores well in the freezer.

¼ cup	olive oil
2 cups	fresh parsley leaves, tightly packed
2 cups	fresh basil leaves, tightly packed
18 cloves	garlic

In a food processor, puree all ingredients, stopping occasionally to scrape sides with a rubber spatula, until well combined. Divide into thirds in three small baby food or glass jars. Store one jar in the refrigerator for immediate use. Store the remaining two jars in the freezer for later use as needed.

If you are using a blender, add the oil first, then garlic (only this time pressed). Add a handful of herbs at a time, blending well after each addition, until all of herbs are used. If ingredients become too thick, you may find it necessary to add up to another tablespoon of olive oil. On occasion, stop the blender and push herbs down past the blade with handle of a wooden spoon until thoroughly blended. Makes 3 small jars of paste.

Ten Ingredient Salad
with Herb Dressing

We are big salad fans and eat salad almost every day. It is very time consuming to wash, cut and prepare salad fixings, so we created a salad that takes a couple of hours to make, but lasts the rest of the week (unless you plan to serve this salad to a large group). After combining all the salad ingredients, place in plastic bags and store in the refrigerator. Use only the amount needed for each salad.

1	**bunch spinach**
1	**bunch Butter lettuce**
1	**bunch Red Leaf lettuce**
1	**head green cabbage (small)**
2 cups	**mushrooms, sliced**
1	**bunch radishes, sliced**
1	**cucumber, thinly sliced**
6	**roma tomatoes, sliced**
1	**red onion, diced**
2	**carrots, shredded**

Wash and trim spinach, Butter lettuce and Red Leaf lettuce. Dry the greens well with paper towel or salad spinner.

In a very large salad bowl, tear spinach, Butter lettuce and Red leaf lettuce into bite-size pieces. Toss to evenly combine.

With a sharp knife, shred cabbage into thin strips and add to lettuce. Add remaining vegetables, tossing after each addition.

In a salad bowl, place desired amount of salad and top with Creamy Italian Dressing (or your favorite dressing). Store the remaining salad in plastic bags for up to one week. Makes 10-15 servings.

Italian Herb Dressing

¼ cup	white vinegar
¾ cup	olive oil
1 tbsp	pesto paste (see recipe page 20)
½ tsp	Italian seasoning
1 tsp	salt
1	egg yolk
2 tbsp	mayonnaise
2 tbsp	sour cream

Combine all ingredients in a blender and mix until smooth and creamy.

Wilted Spinach Salad with Hot French Dressing

2	bunches spinach, washed, trimmed and dried
2 cups	mushrooms, sliced
1	basket cherry tomatoes, halved
¹/₂ cup	red onion, diced
3	hard boiled eggs, sliced

In a large salad bowl, tear spinach into bite-size pieces. Add mushrooms, tomatoes and red onion. Toss to combine. Crumble eggs over top of salad.

Pour Hot French Dressing (recipe follows) over salad a little at a time (beat the dressing as you pour, as spices tend to fall to the bottom of the pan when the oil is heated) and toss after each addition until spinach is coated. Makes 4 large or 8 small salads.

Hot French Dressing

¹/₂ cup	vinegar
³/₄ tsp	salt
¹/₄ tsp	white pepper
1 clove	garlic, pressed
1 tsp	dry mustard
¹/₂ tsp	thyme
1 tbsp	fresh chives, finely chopped
1¹/₂ cup	olive oil
1 tsp	Pickapeppa sauce

Combine all ingredients in a blender and mix thoroughly. Pour into a small sized saucepan and place over high heat until dressing comes to a boil. Immediately pour over spinach salad, beating as you pour.

Garlic Lovers Caesar Salad

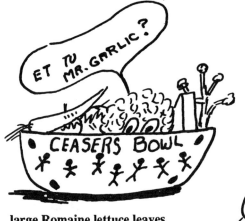

10	large Romaine lettuce leaves
4	large Butter lettuce leaves
2 tbsp	butter
1¹/₂ tbsp	olive oil
4 cloves	garlic, pressed
¹/₂ tsp	garlic salt
4	medium slices french bread
4 oz	fresh Parmesan cheese, grated

Wash and dry lettuce, then tear into bite-size pieces in a large salad bowl.

Melt butter in small saucepan. Stir in oil, garlic, and garlic salt.

Brush french bread slices with the melted garlic butter, and broil until golden brown. Dice bread into bite-sized cubes and sprinkle on top of lettuce.

Sprinkle Parmesan cheese over salad, then pour on the Caesar Salad Dressing (recipe follows). Toss gently to mix well. Makes 2 large, or 4 small salads.

Caesar Salad Dressing

1	egg	2 tsp	White Wine Worces-
4 cloves	garlic		tershire Sauce
3 tbsp	olive oil	¹/₃ tsp	salt
2¹/₂ tbsp	lemon juice	¹/₂ tsp	black pepper
1 tbsp	Dijon mustard		

Combine all ingredients in a blender and mix thoroughly.

Oriental Salad With Peanut Dressing

1	head iceberg lettuce
½ head	green cabbage
2 cups	bean sprouts
1	bunch scallions, chopped
20	won ton wrapper sheets
2 cups	vegetable oil for deep frying

Slice lettuce and cabbage in long, thin strips and mix together. Wash and dry bean sprouts, then add to lettuce with scallions.

To make fried won ton strips, take 20 sheets of won ton wrapper and cut into approximately ¼ inch strips. Set aside. Pour vegetable oil into a medium saucepan and place on high heat. Drop one strip of won ton (as a tester) into the oil. When the won ton strip starts to bubble, reduce the heat to medium and remove the tester strip. Drop about 10 strips of won ton in hot oil and fry until light, golden brown. Remove with a slotted spoon or spatula onto a plate covered with paper towel. Repeat this procedure until all the won ton strips are used.

Make the Peanut Dressing (recipe follows) and pour desired amount over lettuce. Toss well, and top with fried won ton strips. Makes 4 large or 6 small salads.

Peanut Dressing

¹/₄ cup	rice vinegar
¹/₈ cup +	
1 tbsp	soy sauce
¹/₄ cup	sesame oil
¹/₂ cup	peanut oil
2 tbsp	peanut butter
2 cloves	garlic, pressed
¹/₈ tsp	cayenne pepper (optional, or to taste)
2	slices ginger, minced
2 tbsp	honey or brown sugar

Combine all ingredients in a blender and mix thoroughly. Heat dressing in a microwave or saucepan until luke warm, before serving.

Potatoes and Greens with Creamy Garlic-Mustard Dressing

RED POTATOES

HERB GARLIC

-M.FALCO-

1	large russet potato
3	small red potatoes
2 cups	Green Leaf lettuce, torn into bite-sized pieces
2 cups	Red Leaf lettuce, torn into bite-sized pieces
4	scallions, chopped
2	medium sized mushrooms, chopped
1	large tomato, chopped
1/3 cup	mayonnaise
2/3 tsp	salt

Scrub all potatoes thoroughly and cut russets to size of red potatoes. Place potatoes in boiling water and cook until fork-tender; let cool. Dice potatoes into medium bite-sized cubes and place in a large mixing bowl. Toss in the scallions, mushrooms, mayonnaise and salt. Mix well until the potatoes are evenly coated.

In a medium sized bowl, toss the lettuce with tomatoes. Divide and evenly place the lettuce and tomato mixture onto 3 large plates. Top with two scoops of potato mixture on each. Drizzle Creamy Garlic Dressing (recipe follows) over all and serve. Makes 3 large salads.

Creamy Garlic-Mustard Dressing

5 cloves	garlic, pressed
1/4 cup	olive oil
1 tbsp	water
2 tbsp	lemon juice
2 tbsp	mayonnaise
1 tsp	Dijon mustard
1/2 tsp	dried oregano leaves
1/4 tsp	black pepper

Place all ingredients in a blender and mix thoroughly. Drizzle over potatoes and greens.

Mixed Vegetable Salad With Hot Curry Dressing

2	red potatoes
1 cup	cauliflower pieces
1 cup	broccoli pieces
1 1/2 cups	Red Leaf lettuce, torn into bite-sized pieces
1 1/2 cups	Green Leaf lettuce, torn into bite-sized pieces
1/2 cup	red onion, diced

Scrub potatoes thoroughly. Place potatoes in boiling water and cook until fork-tender. Let cool. Dice potatoes into medium bite-sized cubes.

Place cauliflower and broccoli in a medium sized saucepan. Add 1/2 cup water. Cook over high heat until water boils. Reduce heat to low. Cover and simmer about 10 minutes until tender. Strain in a colander, and let cool about 5 minutes.

In a large salad bowl, gently toss together all the ingredients. Top with desired amount of Hot Curry Dressing (recipe follows). Toss well and serve. Makes 2-3 servings.

Hot Curry Dressing

6 tbsp	**olive oil**
4 tbsp	**mayonnaise**
2 tbsp	**vinegar**
2 tsp	**curry powder**
2 tsp	**honey**
1 tsp	**salt**
½ tsp	**black pepper**

Place all ingredients in a blender and blend until smooth and creamy. (For a less spicy dressing, reduce curry powder to 1 teaspoon.) Pour over Mixed Vegetable Salad.

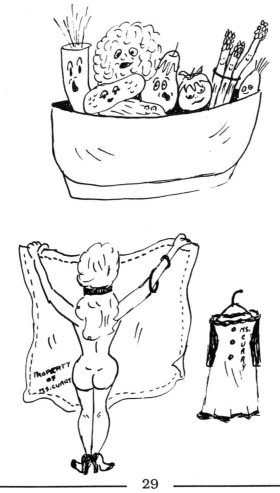

Spicy Potato Salad

— M. FALCO —

4	medium russet potatoes
6	small red potatoes
1	onion, chopped
2	celery stalks, chopped
3	mushrooms, chopped
2	dill pickles, diced
¾ cup	mayonnaise
2½ tbsp	Dijon mustard
1 tsp	thyme
½ tsp	marjoram
1 tsp	salt
½ tsp	pepper
¼ tsp	cayenne pepper
¼ tsp	white pepper

Scrub all potatoes thoroughly and cut russets to size of red potatoes. Place potatoes in boiling water and cook until fork-tender; let cool. Dice potatoes into medium bite-sized cubes and place in a large mixing bowl. (Leaving the peeling on potatoes is optional.)

In a small mixing bowl, stir together the remaining 12 ingredients; pour over potatoes and gently toss until well mixed. Makes 6-8 servings.

Honey Mustard Coleslaw

1¼ cups	mayonnaise
1 tbsp	milk
1 tbsp	lemon juice
2 tbsp	honey
2 tsp	Dijon mustard
¼ tsp	salt
⅛ tsp	paprika
⅛ tsp	ground mustard
1	medium head green cabbage, finely grated
2	carrots, grated
½ cup	red onion, chopped finely

In a blender, mix mayonnaise, milk, lemon juice, honey, mustard, salt, paprika and ground mustard until well blended and smooth.

In a large bowl, gently toss cabbage, carrots, red onion and dressing. Cover and refrigerate. Makes 8 servings.

Cold Green Bean Salad

3 cups	fresh green beans, cut into 1 inch lengths
2 cups	mushrooms, sliced
4	roma tomatoes, sliced
1 tsp	pesto paste (see recipe page 20)

Place green beans in a saucepan and cover with water. Add the pesto paste. Place on high heat and bring to a boil. Reduce heat to medium and continue to cook until the beans are tender, but still firm. (Approx. 10-15 minutes.) Strain beans in colander. Run cold water over them until they have cooled down. Pat dry.

Place cooled beans in a medium sized serving bowl. Add in the sliced mushrooms and tomatoes. Pour Creamy Dill Dressing (recipe follows) over salad and mix well. Refrigerate until ready to serve. Toss once just before serving. Makes approximately 4 servings.

Creamy Dill Dressing

1	egg yolk
1/2 cup	mayonnaise
1/4 cup	sour cream
1/2 tsp	dill weed
1/2 tsp	pesto paste (see recipe page 20)
1/4 tsp	Spike All Purpose Seasoning

Combine all ingredients in a blender and mix thoroughly

Easy Pesto Salad

⅓ cup	olive oil
2 tsp	pesto paste (see recipe page 20)
¼ tsp	salt
1 tbsp	fresh lime or lemon juice
1 pinch	white pepper
1	cucumber, sliced into ¼ inch thick slices
3	medium sized tomatoes sliced into ¼ inch thick slices
7	slices Muenster cheese, cut into 2 inch strips, or cut into decorative shapes with cookie dough cutter. (Cut two shapes on each slice)

Combine olive oil, pesto paste, salt, lemon juice and white pepper in a blender. Mix well. Place in refrigerator until ready to serve.

Alternate cucumber, tomatoes and cheese slices in a row on a medium sized serving dish, overlapping the slices. Should make approx. 3 rows. Drizzle Pesto Sauce over top and serve. Makes 6 servings.

Spicy Hot Pasta Salad

1 tbsp	butter
½ tsp	salt
12 oz	package Rotini noodles (twisted)
2 tbsp	white sesame seeds
2 tbsp	Mongolian Fire oil (or hot oil)
2 tbsp	soy sauce
3 tbsp	red wine vinegar
2 tsp	sugar
¼ tsp	ground ginger
2 cloves	garlic, pressed
¼ cup	peanut oil
1 cup	green cabbage, thinly sliced
¼ cup	red bell pepper, diced

Fill a large saucepan with water. Add butter and salt; bring to a boil. Stir in noodles; cook 6-7 minutes until tender. Drain in colander.

In a blender, combine the sesame seeds, hot oil, soy sauce, vinegar, sugar, ground ginger, garlic cloves and peanut oil. Blend until well combined.

In a salad bowl, toss the Rotini noodles, cabbage and red pepper. Pour the dressing over the salad and toss well. Refrigerate until ready to serve. Makes 6-8 servings.

-M. FALCO-

Fresh Fruit Salad with Lemon Yogurt Dressing

2	red apples
2	bananas
2 tbsp	lemon juice
2	oranges
4 cups	fresh strawberries, halved
2 cups	fresh pineapple chunks
1 cup	fresh blueberries
12 oz.	lemon flavored yogurt

Peel apples, then quarter and remove core and seeds. Chop into small pieces. Slice bananas $1/4$ inch thick. Place apples and bananas in a medium sized bowl. Add lemon juice and gently toss, making sure to cover all fruit. Set aside.

Peel the oranges and remove as much of the white skin as possible. Slice into $1/4$ inch thick pieces, and then into quarters. In a large serving bowl, gently toss together all fruit, including bowl of apples and bananas. Gently stir in yogurt. Wrap and refrigerate until ready to serve. Toss once just before serving.

Makes 6-8 servings.

Holiday Cranberry Fruit Salad

12 oz	fresh cranberries
$^1/_2$ cup	fresh orange juice
$^1/_2$ cup	honey
13	whole dates, pitted
$1^1/_2$ tsp	grated orange peel
1 cup	frozen raspberries, thawed
$1^1/_2$ cups	green seedless grapes, halved
2	red or green apples, cored and cut into small pieces
4	kiwi fruits, peeled and sliced

In a food processor or blender, finely chop cranberries. Place into a medium sized bowl.

In a blender, add orange juice, honey and dates. Blend until dates are chopped very fine and mixture becomes thick and creamy.

Stir orange and date mixture into cranberries, along with orange peel and raspberries. Cover and let set in refrigerator for at least one hour, in order for the flavors to blend. Next, stir in apples and half of the grapes.

Just before serving, gently stir in half of the kiwi slices. Transfer the fruit salad into a serving bowl, then decoratively top with remaining grape halves and kiwi slices.

Makes 6-8 servings.

Soups & Casseroles

Vege-Tom Soup

8	medium sized tomatoes
3 tbsp	butter
3	mushrooms, chopped
1 cup	onions, chopped
1 cup	zucchini, diced
2	medium carrots, diced
2	stalks celery, sliced
1 cup	fresh or frozen peas
5 cups	water
2	vegetable bouillon cubes
12 oz	can tomato paste
1/2 cup	heavy or whipping cream
1/4 cup	parsley, finely chopped
1/2 tsp	Lemon & Pepper Seasoning Salt
1 tsp	salt
1/4 tsp	black pepper
1/8 tsp	cayenne pepper
1/2 tsp	garlic salt
1/2 tsp	marjoram
1/2 tsp	cilantro (coriander leaf)

Fill a large saucepan with water and bring to a boil. Drop tomatoes in and let boil approximately 1 minute or until skins start to break. Remove tomatoes from water and let sit until cool enough to handle. With a knife, peel skin from tomato. Chop tomatoes into large pieces; set aside.

In a large saucepan, melt butter over medium-high heat. Add mushrooms, onion, zucchini, carrots and celery. Sauté until tender. Add the water and bouillon cubes. Stir until bouillon dissolves. Stir in the tomato paste, cream, parsley, chopped tomato and all spices. Bring to a boil, then reduce heat. Cover, and let simmer for 1 hour. Stir occasionally and mash tomato pieces until they are incorporated into the soup. Add the peas and cook until heated through. Makes 6-10 servings.

Creamy Mushroom Soup

2 lbs	mushrooms, washed
³/₄ cup	butter
2¹/₂ tsp	salt
1	medium onion, chopped (approx. 1¹/₂ cups)
1 cup	heavy or whipping cream
¹/₂ cup	flour
3 cups	milk
¹/₂ cup	Cabernet Sauvignon wine (or your favorite dry red wine)
1 tsp	white pepper
1 tsp	black pepper
¹/₂ cup	sour cream

Remove stems from mushrooms; chop and place in a bowl along with onions and set aside. Slice mushroom caps into ¹/₄ inch thick slices.

In a large saucepan, melt butter. Add 1 teaspoon salt and the sliced mushroom caps. Sauté over medium-high heat until mushrooms are tender. Reduce heat to medium-low. With a slotted spoon, remove cooked mushrooms and place in a separate bowl, leaving liquid in saucepan.

Add the mushroom stems and onion to liquid; cook until onions are tender. While the stems and onion are cooking, purée 2 cups of the sauteed mushroom caps with the cream in a food processor or blender; set aside.

With a whisk, stir flour into simmering onions and mushrooms until blended. Cook 1 minute stirring constantly. Gradually stir in milk, wine, remaining 1½ teaspoon salt, black and white pepper. Raise heat to medium-high. Cook, stirring constantly, until mixture is slightly thickened (10-15 minutes).

Stir in the pureed mushrooms, and the remaining sliced mushrooms. Heat just until boils.

Remove from heat and stir in sour cream. Serve immediately. Makes approximately 6 servings.

Cream of Broccoli Soup

2	bunches broccoli (6 stalks)
1 cup	water
2 tsp	pesto paste (see recipe page 20)
3 cups	milk
⅓ cup	flour
¼ cup	butter
1 tbsp	lemon peel, grated
1 cup	onion, chopped
1 tsp	Lemon and Herb seasoning
1 tsp	Lemon Pepper seasoning
½ tsp	white pepper
2 tsp	salt

Cut off the tops of broccoli. With a knife, remove the thick outer skin from the stalks. Coarsely chop all the broccoli and place in a medium sized saucepan. Add 1 cup water, and 1 teaspoon of the pesto paste. Cook over high heat until water boils. Reduce heat to low. Cover and simmer about 10 minutes until tender. Strain in a colander, and let cool about 5 minutes.

Add 1 cup milk and the cooked broccoli into a food processor or blender. Purée and set aside.

In a small bowl, combine flour and 1 cup milk. Stir until smooth, removing all lumps. Set aside.

In a large saucepan, sauté the lemon peel and onion in butter, until the onion is tender. Pour in the flour and milk mixture, stirring constantly until thickened. Turn heat to medium-low. With a whisk, stir in remaining 1 cup milk. Add all the spices, and remaining 1 teaspoon pesto paste while continuing to stir. Pour in the broccoli purée and stir well. Raise heat to medium-high. Stir constantly until soup just begins to boil. Remove from heat and serve. Makes 4-5 servings.

Cream of Potato and Cheese Soup

6	russet potatoes
3 tbsp	butter
1	medium sized onion, chopped
2 tbsp	flour
4 cups	milk
3 cups	sharp cheddar cheese, grated
1 tsp	garlic salt
1 tsp	white pepper
1/2 tsp	black pepper
1 1/2 tsp	salt
1 tsp	onion powder
1/2 tsp	ground cumin seed
1/2 tsp	whole celery seed
2	vegetable bouillon cubes
4 cups	water

Scrub all potatoes thoroughly. In a large saucepan, cover potatoes with water and boil until fork-tender. Let cool, then peel and chop the potatoes in large cubes. Set aside.

In a medium sized bowl, pour 4 cups boiling water over bouillon cubes. Let cubes sit until dissolved.

In a large skillet, melt butter. Add the onions and sauté until just tender. With a whisk, stir in the flour, then 2 cups of milk. Stir constantly until mixture starts to thicken and there are no lumps. Stir in the cheese until melted, then add remaining 2 cups milk. Stir in the following 7 spices, then the bouillon liquid.

Purée the potatoes and soup mixture in a food processor or blender. Return soup to large saucepan and heat through. Serve immediately. Makes 6-10 servings.

Lemon Grass Soup

2 cups	dried lemon grass
10 cups	water
1/4 cup	butter
1 tbsp	Lemon & Pepper Seasoning Salt
2	medium sized potatoes, diced
3	carrots, diced
2	celery stalks, sliced
1	bunch scallions, including greens, finely chopped
2	vegetarian vegetable bouillon cubes
1 tsp	salt
1/2 tsp	white pepper

In a medium sized saucepan, add lemon grass to 5 cups of water and bring to a boil. Reduce heat so water is just boiling; cover and let simmer 1 hour. In a bowl, strain the liquid from lemon grass. Discard the lemon grass and place liquid aside until called for.

In a large saucepan, melt the butter. Add Lemon & Pepper Seasoning, potatoes, carrots and celery stalks. Sauté until all vegetables are just tender. Stir in the scallions, remaining 5 cups of water, lemon grass liquid, bouillon cubes, salt and pepper. Cover, and let simmer 30 minutes, stirring occasionally. Makes 6-10 servings.

LEMON GRASS PATCH

Potato Casserole

7	medium potatoes
1/2 cup	butter
2 tsp	salt
1 tsp	dried parsley
1/4 tsp	white pepper
1 1/4 cup	plain bread crumbs (fine)
2 cups	Muenster cheese, grated

Place potatoes and 1 teaspoon salt in boiling water and cook until fork-tender. Drain potatoes and let cool. With a knife, peel and dice potatoes.

In a small skillet, melt 1/4 cup of the butter. Add 1 teaspoon salt, parsley and pepper. Put the diced potatoes in a large salad bowl Pour butter over the potatoes and toss. In a large skillet over medium-high heat, melt remaining 1/4 cup butter until bubbly. Add the bread crumbs and mix until crumbs are evenly coated. Remove pan from heat.

Layer the bottom of a large casserole dish with potatoes until just covered. Sprinkle with Muenster cheese, then a generous amount of bread crumb mixture. Repeat layers ending with bread crumbs.

Cover with foil and bake in a 425° oven for 15 minutes. Remove the foil and continue baking 10 minutes uncovered. Makes 8-10 servings.

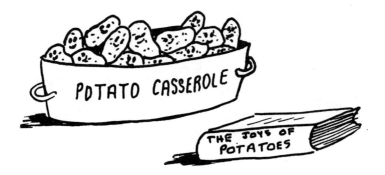

Macaroni and Cheese Casserole with Mini Veggie Burger Balls

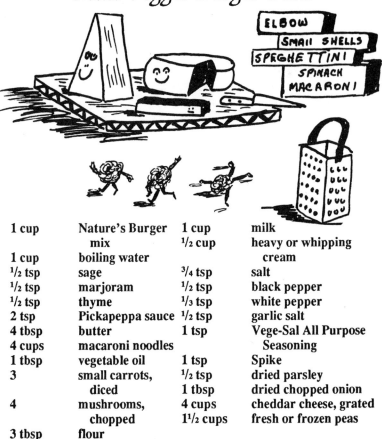

1 cup	Nature's Burger mix	1 cup	milk
1 cup	boiling water	½ cup	heavy or whipping cream
½ tsp	sage	¾ tsp	salt
½ tsp	marjoram	½ tsp	black pepper
½ tsp	thyme	⅓ tsp	white pepper
2 tsp	Pickapeppa sauce	½ tsp	garlic salt
4 tbsp	butter	1 tsp	Vege-Sal All Purpose Seasoning
4 cups	macaroni noodles		
1 tbsp	vegetable oil	1 tsp	Spike
3	small carrots, diced	½ tsp	dried parsley
		1 tbsp	dried chopped onion
4	mushrooms, chopped	4 cups	cheddar cheese, grated
		1½ cups	fresh or frozen peas
3 tbsp	flour		

Stir boiling water into Nature's Burger mix along with sage, marjoram, thyme, and Pickapeppa sauce. Let sit 7-10 minutes. Form the mixture into small mini balls, about the size of a large marble.

In a large skillet over medium-high heat, melt 2 tablespoons of the butter. Add the burger balls, and fry until browned on all sides. Set aside.

Fill a medium sized saucepan half full with water. Bring to a boil. Add macaroni noodles and oil. Boil noodles until tender. Drain. Set aside.

In a large saucepan over medium-high heat, melt remaining 2 tablespoons butter. Stir in carrots and mushrooms. Sauté until vegetables are tender. Stir in the flour and milk with a whisk, beating vigorously until smooth. Stir in cream, and the next 8 spices. Add in the cheese and cook while still stirring, until cheese just melts. Remove pan from heat. Stir in frozen peas and cooked macaroni noodles, then gently fold in burger balls.

Turn the macaroni mixture into a large casserole dish. Bake in a 375° oven for 15-20 minutes until heated through. Makes 6-8 servings.

Sandwiches

Sassy Salsa Burraco

4	flour tortillas
2 tbsp	butter
2	avocados, sliced
2	large dill pickles, sliced thin
1 cup	tomatoes, diced
1 cup	onion, diced
2 cups	alfalfa sprouts
8 tbsp	salsa (see recipe page 18 or use your favorite brand)

In a frying pan over medium high heat, melt 1 tablespoon butter. Heat flour tortillas until they are a light golden brown, adding more butter to pan as needed.

Put flour tortilla on a plate and add $^1/_2$ sliced avocado, $^1/_2$ sliced dill pickle, $^1/_4$ cup tomatoes, $^1/_4$ cup onion, and $^1/_2$ cup alfalfa sprouts to the middle. Then drizzle over the top approximately 2 tablespoons (or as much as you like) salsa. Repeat procedure until you have filled all four tortillas.

Roll the tortilla burrito style, and place a toothpick in the center to hold together. Makes 4 servings.

Falafil Cone With
Sweet and Sour Dressing

Falafil is a hardy protein food made from beans, peas, wheat germ and spices; a favorite of Middle Easterners for over one thousand years. It is kept in a dry form, stores well and is easily prepared. Together with our Sweet and Sour Dressing, this cone style sandwich becomes a gourmet meal. (Falafil can usually be found at your grocer in the dry food section.)

1 cup	Falafil mix
2/3 cup	cold water
	vegetable oil (for deep frying)
4	whole-wheat tortillas, or chapati
1 1/2 cups	lettuce, shredded
3/4 cup	onion, diced
8	medium slices tomato

Mix water with Falafil mix and let stand for 15 minutes. Scoop a scant 1/8 cup of mix, and roll into a ball. Continue, making a total of 12 balls.

Pour at least 1 inch of vegetable oil into a deep fryer or other pan. Heat oil to approximately 350° to 375° F. Fry Falafil balls until brown and crisp. Drain on paper towels.

Heat tortillas on hot dry skillet until they are soft but not crisp.

To assemble, shape each tortilla into the shape of a cone; folding bottom point up 1/4 inch. Wrap a piece of foil or napkin around the bottom of cone to hold together. This keeps any liquid from dripping through. With the seam side up, hold the cone horizontally while layering bottom side evenly with some shredded lettuce. Next layer 2 tablespoons diced onion, and 2 slices tomato. Stuff 3 Falafil balls into the middle of each cone. Pour a generous amount of Sweet and Sour Dressing (recipe follows) over top, and let drizzle down into the cone. Serve immediately. Makes 4 servings.

Sweet and Sour Dressing

1 cup	sour cream
1 tbsp	fresh lime juice
$1/2$ tsp	dill weed
$1/4$ cup	mayonnaise
1 tbsp	milk
$1/8$ tsp	salt
1 tsp	honey

Place all ingredients in a blender and mix until thoroughly combined. Let sit 5-10 minutes before serving, to allow flavors time to blend.

Quick Sourdough C-L-T's

4 slices	sourdough bread
8 slices	cheddar cheese (medium thick)
8 slices	tomato
4-8	lettuce leaves
	mayonnaise to taste

Spread desired amount of mayonnaise on all the bread slices. On 2 slices of bread layer 4 slices of cheese, 4 slices tomato and 2-4 lettuce leaves on each. Top with remaining bread slices, cut in half and serve.

2 servings.

Extra Tasty Grilled Tomato and Cheese Sandwich

We have two things to say about this sandwich. One, the spicy mustard we recommend is one of the main reasons for its success, and two, **yum!**

8 slices	**whole-wheat bread**
8	**thick slices tomato**
4	**slices sharp cheddar cheese (sandwich sized)**
4	**crisp lettuce leaves**
	mayonnaise, to taste
	Grey Poupon Dijon Mustard (made with white wine), to taste
	Vege-Sal All Purpose Seasoning, to taste

Lightly toast bread, and place evenly on a baking sheet lined with foil.

Spread mayonnaise on 4 slices of bread. Top each with two slices of tomato.

On remaining slices of bread, spread Dijon mustard and top each with cheese. Sprinkle Vege-Sal All Purpose Seasoning over cheese, and set in a broiler until cheese is melted. Remove from broiler and top with crisp lettuce leaves.

Fold the cheese and tomato sections together. Cut in half and serve. Makes 4 servings.

Veggie Monsters

And we thought being vegetarians was going to be boring! This tasty sandwich would convert the most hardened criminal. It is **good!**

8 slices	whole-wheat bread
1	large avocado, cut into 12 even slices
8	medium tomato slices
4	full sized red onion slices
½ cup	mayonnaise
2 tbsp	Dijon mustard
3	medium size mushrooms, chopped
2 cups	cheddar cheese, grated
1 tsp	Vege-Sal All Purpose Seasoning
1 cup	alfalfa sprouts

Arrange the bread slices evenly on a cutting board. Layer 3 slices avocado, 2 slices tomato, and 1 slice onion on each of 4 of the bread slices.

In a saucepan, add mayonnaise, mustard, mushrooms, cheese, and Vege-Sal All Purpose Seasoning. Stir over medium heat until just melted. Spoon evenly over prepared bread slices.

Top each with ¼ cup alfalfa sprouts and remaining wheat bread. Enjoy! Makes 4 servings.

Stuffed Pita Monsters
with Monster Sauce

Why the catchy name? Simply because they're a monster of a sandwich!

1 cup	**Nature's Burger**
1 cup	**boiling water**
2 tsp	**Pickapeppa sauce**
$^1/_2$ tsp	**garlic salt**
$^1/_4$ tsp	**black pepper**
$^1/_4$ tsp	**cayenne pepper**
1 tbsp	**butter**
4	**pita breads, cut open but not in half**
1	**avocado, cut into 12 slices**
8	**slices tomato**
1 cup	**alfalfa sprouts**

Mix Nature's Burger with boiling water, Pickapeppa sauce, and spices. Let mixture set 10 minutes. Form 4 patties and fry in butter until golden brown on both sides.

Place a patty into each of the pita breads, and top with a generous amount of Monster Sauce (recipe follows), 3 avocado slices, 2 tomato slices, and $^1/_4$ cup sprouts. Makes 4 servings.

Monster Sauce

$1^1/_2$ cups	**cheese of your choice, grated**
$^1/_2$	**onion, chopped**
$^1/_3$ cup	**mayonnaise**
2 tbsp	**Dijon mustard**
$^1/_2$ tsp	**Vege-Sal All Purpose Seasoning**

In a medium size saucepan, stir all ingredients together over low heat until cheese melts.

Extra Large Sourdough Veggie Burger Sandwiches

1¹/₂ cups	Nature's Burger
1¹/₂ cups	boiling water
1 tsp	salt
2 tsp	Pickapeppa sauce
2 tbsp	butter
8 slices	sourdough bread
1 cup	onion, diced
1 cup	Swiss cheese, grated
¹/₂ tsp	black pepper
¹/₂ tsp	white pepper
³/₄ tsp	Vege-Sal All Purpose Seasoning
12-16	slices tomato
4	large lettuce leaves
	mayonnaise to taste
	Dijon mustard to taste

In a medium sized bowl stir boiling water into Nature's Burger mix. Add the salt and Pickapeppa sauce; stir well. Let sit for 10 minutes, then form mixture into 6 small patties. In a large skillet, fry 3 of the patties at a time in 1 tablespoon butter, until each side is golden brown.

Arrange the sourdough slices on a cutting board. Spread desired amount of mayonnaise on half the slices and Dijon mustard on the remaining half.

In a medium sized saucepan over medium-low heat, melt remaining 1 tablespoon butter. Add the onions and sauté until soft. Stir in the Swiss cheese, black and white pepper, and Vege-Sal All Purpose Seasoning. Stir constantly until cheese is thoroughly melted.

Cut two of the Nature's Burger patties in half. Place 1^1/$_2$ patties on each of the sourdough slices spread with mayonnaise. Top with 3-4 slices tomatoes (depending on your taste) and 1 large lettuce leaf.

Spoon a generous amount of the grilled onion and cheese mixture onto the remaining sourdough slices. Fold the halves together and enjoy! Makes 4 extra large sandwiches.

Foot-Long Vegamarines

Dedicated to those hard working men who thought being a vegetarian wouldn't conquer their appetite.

2	**foot-long french rolls**
8 slices	**Swiss cheese**
6 slices	**cheddar cheese**
4 slices	**onion, cut in half**
8 slices	**tomatoes**
1	**dill pickle, cut lengthwise into 6 slices**
1	**avocado, cut into 12 slices**
1 cup	**lettuce, shredded**
	mayonnaise to taste
	Dijon mustard to taste
	Spike Seasoning to taste

Cut french rolls in half lengthwise, arrange all halves on a cookie sheet lined with foil.

Spread desired amount of Dijon mustard on bottom halves of french rolls. Alternately layer 4 slices of the Swiss cheese with 3 slices of cheddar cheese (starting and ending with Swiss cheese). Sprinkle with Spike Seasoning. Next, spread desired amount of mayonnaise on the top french roll halves. In order, layer 3 slices pickles, 6 slices avocados, 4 slices tomatoes and 4 half slices onions on each.

Place all the sandwich halves under the broiler for about 1 minute, or until the halves with cheese melt.

Spread $1/2$ cup shredded lettuce on top of each cheese half. Evenly pour Vegamarine Dressing (recipe follows) over lettuce. Fold halves together and serve warm. Makes 2-4 servings.

Vegamarine Dressing

2 tbsp	olive oil
1 tbsp	vinegar
$1/4$ tsp	pepper
$1/4$ tsp	salt
$1/2$	fresh jalapeño pepper

Place all the ingredients in a blender and blend thoroughly. Pour evenly over lettuce on Vegamarine sandwiches.

Sunk-in Italian Vegaball Sandwiches

1½ cups	Nature's Burger mix
1¼ cups	boiling water
1 tbsp	Pickapeppa sauce
15 oz	can tomato sauce
6 oz	can Italian tomato paste
1 tbsp	dry red wine
5 cloves	garlic, pressed
½ tsp	thyme
⅓ tsp	oregano
¼ tsp	salt
¼ tsp	black pepper
½ tsp	garlic salt
¼ tsp	cayenne pepper
3 tbsp	butter
4	foot-long french rolls
16	slices Mozarella cheese
4½ oz	can sliced ripe olives
16	slices tomato
3 cups	lettuce, shredded

Stir boiling water into Nature's Burger mix. Add the Pickapeppa sauce and mix well. Let sit 10 minutes.

In a medium sized saucepan over medium heat, add the tomato sauce, tomato paste, wine, garlic and other 6 spices. Bring sauce to a boil, then reduce heat to low. Cover, and let simmer 10-15 minutes.

Roll the Nautre's Burger mixture into 12 small meat-less balls. Fry in a skillet with 1 tablespoon butter until browned on all sides.

Cut the french rolls in half lengthwise. Working carefully with a knife, remove most of the bread from the bottom half of the rolls, leaving $1/2$ inch on the bottom and sides. Fill with 3 vegaballs, several spoonfuls of sauce, and 4 slices mozzarella cheese. Arrange on a baking sheet lined with foil. Place the top halves of rolls upside down on baking sheet; lightly spread with the other 2 tablespoons of butter.

Place the rolls under broiler. Broil until cheese is melted, and top halves are a light golden brown. Place 4 slices of tomato on each of the bottom rolls, then evenly layer on the lettuce. Add on top roll and serve while still warm. Makes 4-8 servings.

Oriental Stir-Fry Burrito's

(Trust us!)

2	medium size carrots
2	medium size broccoli stalks
1/2	medium size yellow squash
3	scallions, finely chopped
1/4 cup	red bell pepper, diced
1/2 cup	soy sauce
1 1/2 tsp	corn starch
1 tbsp	ketchup
2 tbsp	brown sugar
2 tbsp	sesame oil
1 clove	garlic, minced
2 tsp	fresh ginger, minced
1 tbsp	sesame seeds
4	flour tortillas

Prepare the vegetables. Diagonally slice carrots 1/4 inch thick, and cut 2 inches in length. Cut or break the tops of broccoli into flowerets. With a knife or peeler, remove thick outer skin on broccoli stems and cut diagonally into bite-size pieces. Cut yellow squash into 1/4 inch thick slices. Separately place all vegetables on a large plate or in individual bowls. Set aside.

In a small cup, stir cornstarch into soy sauce until corn starch dissolves. Stir in the ketchup and brown sugar. Set aside.

In a large saucepan or skillet, heat the sesame oil on medium-high heat. Add the garlic, ginger and sesame seeds. Cook for about 30 seconds or until sesame seeds turn a light golden brown. Reduce heat to medium. Add carrots and stir-fry 1 minute. Add broccoli and stir-fry 1 minute. Add squash, bell pepper and onion; stir fry another minute. Stir in the soy sauce mixture and heat until thickened, tossing vegetables to coat well. Reduce heat to medium low, and cook all vegetables 1-2 minutes longer, stirring occasionally until all vegetables are tender-crisp. Remove from heat and let sit while preparing flour tortillas.

In a dry skillet, heat tortillas until softened. Pour $1/2$ cup of the stir-fried vegetables into the center of each tortilla. Fold one side of tortilla up about $1/2$ inch then roll burrito style. Place a toothpick in center to hold together. (It is inevitable that a little sauce will drip through the tortilla, so have plenty of napkins on hand.) Makes 4 burrito's.

Eggs, Cheese & Tofu Dishes

Veggie Omelette

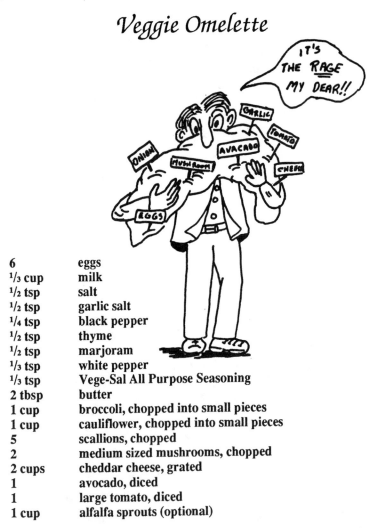

6	eggs
1/3 cup	milk
1/2 tsp	salt
1/2 tsp	garlic salt
1/4 tsp	black pepper
1/2 tsp	thyme
1/2 tsp	marjoram
1/3 tsp	white pepper
1/3 tsp	Vege-Sal All Purpose Seasoning
2 tbsp	butter
1 cup	broccoli, chopped into small pieces
1 cup	cauliflower, chopped into small pieces
5	scallions, chopped
2	medium sized mushrooms, chopped
2 cups	cheddar cheese, grated
1	avocado, diced
1	large tomato, diced
1 cup	alfalfa sprouts (optional)

In a large mixing bowl, beat together the eggs, milk and 7 spices.

In a large oven-proof skillet over medium-low heat, melt butter. Pour in the egg mixture and cook for approximately 1 minute. Sprinkle in broccoli, cauliflower, scallions and mushrooms. Continue to cook for approximately 1 minute. Occasionally push spatula through egg mixture to allow uncooked eggs to seep through. Remove from burner and place under broiler until top of egg mixture turns a light golden brown. Place back on burner, reduce heat to low, and cook for another 30 seconds while sprinkling on cheese. Place back under broiler until cheese melts. Top with diced avocados, tomatoes and alfalfa sprouts. Cut into fourths and serve. Makes 4 servings.

Saucy Pirate Eyes

7 tbsp	butter
1/4 tsp	salt
1/4 tsp	Lemon & Pepper Seasoning Salt
1/4 tsp	white pepper
1 cup	half & half
2	egg yolks
1 cup	cheddar cheese, grated
4 slices	extra large sourdough bread
4	eggs
4	fresh cooked whole artichoke hearts (or marinated)

In a small skillet or saucepan, melt 3 tablespoons of the butter and stir in salt, Lemon & Pepper Seasoning, and white pepper. In a small cup, beat together the half & half and egg yolks. Pour into the melted butter, stirring vigorously until thick and creamy. Add the cheese until just melted. Remove pan from heat and prepare the pirate eyes.

Cut a round hole in the middle of each sourdough slice about three inches in diameter.

In a large skillet over medium heat, melt 1 tablespoon of remaining butter at a time. Place a slice of sourdough in the pan (or as many slices that may fit) then crack an egg into the center of the hole. Cook for approximately 1 minute (or depending on how you like your eggs) on each side.

Place each pirate eye on individual plates. Invert the artichoke heart, placing it over the egg yolk upside down. Pour 1/4 cup cheese sauce over each. Serve hot. Makes 4 servings.

Broccoli and Cheese Quiche

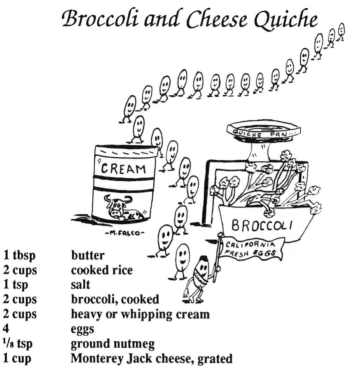

-M. FALCO-

1 tbsp	butter
2 cups	cooked rice
1 tsp	salt
2 cups	broccoli, cooked
2 cups	heavy or whipping cream
4	eggs
1/8 tsp	ground nutmeg
1 cup	Monterey Jack cheese, grated

Melt butter and stir into rice along with 1/4 teaspoon salt. Pat rice in bottom and sides of 9 inch pie plate with the back of a metal spoon. Bake in a 450° oven for 20 minutes.

In a blender, purée the broccoli with cream.

In a medium sized bowl, add eggs, nutmeg and 3/4 teaspoon salt; mix well. Stir in cheese and pureed broccoli.

Pour egg mixture into baked rice shell. Bake in a 425° for 15 minutes; turn oven control to 325°; bake 25 minutes longer or when knife inserted in center comes out clean. Let stand 10 minutes before serving. Makes 6 servings.

Tofu and Egg Scramble

6	eggs
1/3 cup	milk
2 tbsp	butter
5	scallions, chopped
2	medium mushrooms, sliced
1	medium zucchini, chopped
1 tsp	salt
1/4 tsp	black pepper
1/4 tsp	white pepper
1/2 tsp	marjoram
1/2 tsp	thyme
8 oz	package fresh tofu, cut in half-inch cubes

In a medium sized bowl, beat eggs and milk with fork. Set aside.

Melt butter in large skillet over medium heat. Add scallions, mushrooms, zucchini and spices. Lightly sauté for about 1 minute.

Pour egg mixture over sauteed vegetables and continue to cook for about 1 minute. Sprinkle in tofu cubes and gently scramble until eggs are fully cooked. Serve immediately. Makes 2-4 servings.

Delicious with buttered toast and jam!

Eggless Tofu Scramble

2 tbsp	butter
2	medium sized mushrooms, diced
$^1/_2$ cup	onion, diced
$^1/_2$ cup	zucchini, diced
$^1/_2$ tsp	Vege-Sal All Purpose Seasoning
$^1/_2$ tsp	salt
$^1/_2$ tsp	thyme
$^1/_2$ tsp	marjoram
$^1/_4$ tsp	white pepper
$^1/_4$ tsp	black pepper
14.2 oz	package fresh, firm tofu, cut into $^1/_2$ inch cubes
$1^1/_2$ cups	tomatoes, chopped
$1^1/_2$ cups	cheddar cheese, grated
1	ripe avocado, chopped into cubes
1 cup	alfalfa sprouts

Melt butter in a large skillet over medium heat. Add mushrooms, onion, zucchini and the spices. Sauté for 1 minute, then add the tofu. Continue to cook, stirring gently until the vegetables are tender, and tofu is heated through.

Transfer tofu mixture to a shallow baking pan. Evenly spread grated cheese over the top. Place baking pan under a broiler, and broil until cheese melts.

Layer on tomatoes, avocados and alfalfa sprouts and serve. Makes 4 servings.

Great with hot buttered corn tortillas or buttered toast and jam.

If you haven't already been introduced to a product called "Nature's Burger" (by Fantastic Foods) in box or bin, now is the time. We've tried most of the frozen Tofu burgers and other mixes, and found them to be pretty unappetizing. Nature's Burger not only tastes pretty good, but the patties actually stick together and fry like an old-fashioned hamburger! We could have come up with our own mixture, but why mess with success. Several of the following recipes will call for Nature's Burger. We will show you how to creatively use it, in order to re-enjoy some old fashioned favorites the Vegetarian way.

Nature's Burger can be found at your local Health Food Store, or check with your local grocer.

Vegetarian Entrées

Mushroom Stroganoff

4 tbsp	butter
2 cloves	garlic, pressed
4 cups	mushrooms, sliced
1 cup	onion, diced
$^1/_3$ cup	flour
$^1/_2$ tsp	salt
$^1/_4$ tsp	black pepper
1$^1/_2$ cups	milk
2 tbsp	Cabernet Sauvignon wine (or your favorite dry red wine)
2 tsp	Pickapeppa sauce
1 cup	sour cream
6 cups	hot cooked egg noodles

In a large skillet, heat 2 tablespoons butter. Add garlic, mushrooms and onion. Cook until mushrooms and onion are tender. Remove mushroom mixture, leaving liquid in pan. Add remaining 2 tablespoons butter to liquid, and heat until melted. Stir in flour, salt and pepper. Add milk, and beat with whisk until there are no lumps. Cook and stir over medium-high heat until thickened and bubbly. Add the wine, Pickapeppa sauce, sour cream and cooked mushrooms. Heat through, but do not boil. Serve over noodles. Makes 4 servings.

Sloppy Veggie Joe's

1¹/₂ cups	Nature's Burger mix
1¹/₂ cups	boiling water
7-8 cloves	garlic, pressed
¹/₂ tsp	salt
¹/₂ tsp	pepper
2 tsp	Pickapeppa sauce
2 tbsp	butter
1 tbsp	dried chopped onions
¹/₂ cup	catsup
6 oz	can tomato paste
1 tbsp	chili powder
¹/₂ tsp	onion powder
¹/₂ tsp	garlic salt
¹/₂ cup	vinegar
2 tbsp	brown sugar
1¹/₂ cups	water
4	whole-wheat burger buns

In a medium sized mixing bowl, pour boiling water into Nature's Burger mix. Add garlic, salt, pepper and Pickapeppa sauce. Stir and let sit 15 minutes.

In a large skillet or saucepan, stir together the catsup, tomato paste, chili powder, onion powder, garlic salt, vinegar, brown sugar and water. Place on medium-high heat until sauce begins to boil. Reduce heat to medium-low and let simmer 10-15 minutes.

Wrap burger buns in foil and place in a 375° oven for 10-15 minutes.

Form six medium-size patties with the Nature's Burger mixture. With the palm of your hand, press the patties down a little to a medium-thin thickness.

In a large skillet over medium-high heat, melt the butter and fry the patties 3 at a time until brown on both sides. Once cooled, tear patties into bite-size pieces and gently stir into Sloppy Joe sauce. Warm until heated through.

Remove the heated burger buns from oven and arrange open faced onto 4 plates. Scoop a generous amount of Sloppy Joe mixture on top of each bun. Serve immediately. Makes 4 servings.

Veggie Burger Gravy
Over Mashed Potatoes

5	medium sized russet potatoes
1 cup	Nature's Burger mix
1 cup	boiling water
2 tsp	Pickapeppa sauce
6 tbsp	butter
1/2	onion, chopped
2	large mushrooms, chopped
4 tbsp	flour
3 cups	milk
2 tbsp	white wine
1 1/2 tsp	salt
1/2 tsp	black pepper
1 tsp	white pepper
1/2 tsp	garlic salt
1/2 cup	cream

Scrub all potatoes thoroughly. Place potatoes in boiling water and cook until fork-tender. Let cool.

In a medium sized bowl, stir together Nature's Burger mix, boiling water and Pickapeppa sauce. Let sit 7-10 minutes. Pat burger mixture into 4 thin patties.

In a large skillet, fry patties in 1 tablespoon butter until browned on both sides; let cool. Tear or cut patties into small bite-size pieces. Set aside.

In a large skillet, melt 2 tablespoons butter. Add onions and mushrooms; sauté until vegetables are tender. Stir in flour and milk, beating vigorously with a whisk until smooth. Add the wine, $^1/_2$ teaspoon of salt, black and white pepper, and garlic salt. Stir until the gravy is thickened. To keep gravy warm, reduce heat to low and stir occasionally until ready to use. Right before serving, gently stir in the Nature's Burger pieces, and cook until just heated through.

Remove skins from potatoes. Cut potatoes into $^1/_2$ inch cubes and place in a large mixing bowl. With an electric mixer or potato masher, blend in 3 tablespoons butter, 1 teaspoon salt, $^1/_2$ cup milk, and the cream, until the potatoes are creamy.

Place the gravy and mashed potatoes into separate serving bowls and serve. (Goes great with a tossed green salad.) Makes 5-7 servings.

Stuffed Biscuits and Old-Fashioned Gravy

2¹/₂ cups	Bisquick
1¹/₃ cups	milk
3 tbsp	butter
1 cup	zucchini, diced
1 cup	mushrooms, diced
1 cup	onion, diced
1 tsp	salt
1 tsp	white pepper
¹/₂ tsp	garlic salt
¹/₂ tsp	onion powder
2 cups	sharp cheddar cheese, grated

Stir together Bisquick and milk in a large bowl. Pat or roll out the dough to ¹/₄ inch thickness on a floured board. Cut out 12 rounds 3 inches in diameter, and 12 rounds 3¹/₂ inches in diameter. Set aside.

In a medium sized skillet, melt butter and sauté zucchini, mushrooms, and onion until tender. Strain vegetables to remove any liquid; transfer to a medium bowl. Stir in the cheddar cheese.

Arrange 12 of the larger dough rounds on a baking sheet. Spoon 2 tablespoons of vegetable mixture into center of each, then top with smaller dough rounds. Pinch the edges of top and bottom biscuit dough together, so the vegetable mixture is completely enclosed. With your fingers, smooth out the edges. Bake in a 375° oven for 10-12 minutes, or until golden brown. Divide, and place Stuffed Biscuits on individual plates. Top with a generous amount of Old Fashioned Gravy (recipe follows). Makes 4-6 servings.

Old Fashioned Gravy

4 tbsp	butter
1 cup	mushrooms, chopped
1/2 cup	flour
4 cups	milk
1/4 cup	white wine
2/3 tsp	black pepper
1 tsp	white pepper
1 1/2 tsp	salt
1 tsp	garlic salt
3 tsp	dried chopped onion

In a large skillet over medium-high heat, melt butter and sauté mushrooms until tender. Stir in the flour, then milk. With a whisk, stir vigorously until creamy, removing all lumps. Reduce heat to medium-low. Stir in all the remaining spices, and continue to stir until gravy thickens. Pour over Stuffed Biscuits.

Old Fashioned Veggie Burgers

Why didn't McDonald's think of this?

1¹/₂ cups	Nature's Burger mix	¹/₄ tsp	cayenne pepper
1¹/₃ cups	boiling water	2 tbsp	butter
2 tbsp	vegetable oil	6	whole-wheat burger buns
5 cloves	garlic, pressed	6	full slices, red onion
2	medium mushrooms, chopped	6	slices, cheddar cheese (burger size)
		6	crisp lettuce leaves
2 tsp	Pickapeppa sauce		mayonnaise to taste
¹/₂ tsp	salt		Dijon mustard to taste
¹/₂ tsp	garlic salt		catsup to taste
¹/₄ tsp	black pepper		

In a large mixing bowl, add Nature's Burger mix, vegetable oil, garlic, mushrooms, Pickapeppa sauce, spices and boiling water. Stir well, let sit 10 minutes, and then form into 6 thick patties. Wrap whole-wheat buns in foil, and heat in a 275° oven for 10-15 minutes.

In a large skillet over medium-high heat, melt 1 tablespoon butter. Fry 3 patties at a time until brown on both sides. (1 tablespoon butter per 3 patties fried,)

Remove heated buns from oven and turn oven to broil. Arrange the patties on a baking sheet lined with foil. Top each patty with a slice of cheese, and place under broiler until cheese melts. Put 1 patty on each bun, and serve with onion, tomato, lettuce, mayonnaise, mustard and catsup. Makes 6 burgers.

Veggie Shake and Bake

1½ cups	water
¼ cup	white vinegar
¼ cup	red wine vinegar
.19 oz	packet instant vegetable broth
6	medium carrots
7	medium potatoes
2	yellow onions
1 tsp	garlic powder
½ cup	flour
1 tsp	onion powder
½ tsp	salt
¼ tsp	white pepper
1 tbsp	chili powder
1 tbsp	dried parsley flakes
4	whole bay leaves

In a large cup, stir together water, vinegars and vegetable broth. Pour liquid into the bottom of a large roasting pan.

Peel and cut all vegetables into large 2 inch pieces. Cut large ends of carrots in half, so all vegetables are the same size.

Combine flour and all spices, except for bay leaf, into a large plastic or medium paper bag. Shake to mix well. Drop cut vegetables in a few at a time, and shake to coat. Repeat until all vegetables are used. Spread vegetables evenly over liquid in roasting pan. Scatter bay leaves over top. Cover pan with lid or foil, and bake in a 400° oven for 1¼ hours, turning and basting vegetables a few times while cooking.

Transfer cooked vegetables to a large serving bowl or platter. Makes 6-8 servings.

Baked Potato Feast
with Veggies and Cheese Sauce

5	large russet potatoes
1	head cauliflower
2	large stalks broccoli
2	medium sized ripe avocados
1 tbsp	mayonnaise
½ tsp	salt
¼ tsp	pepper
¼ tsp	cayenne pepper
2 tbsp	Pickapeppa sauce
1 cube +	
2 tbsp	butter
1	medium sized zucchini, chopped
½	medium sized onion, chopped
3	medium sized mushrooms, chopped
1 cup	sour cream
½ cup	fresh chives, chopped

Wash and scrub potatoes. Dry, and puncture a few times with a fork. Place on a baking sheet. Bake in a 400° oven for 40 to 60 minutes, depending on size.

Wash cauliflower and broccoli. Cut into medium sized pieces and place in a saucepan with ¹/₂ cup water over high heat. When water comes to a boil, reduce heat to low. Cover and let steam for about 10 minutes, or until vegetables are tender-crisp. Drain in a colander, and place under cold running water until cooled down. Let dry. Set aside.

In a small mixing bowl with electric mixer, blend the avocados, mayonnaise, salt, pepper, cayenne pepper, and Pickapeppa sauce, until smooth and creamy. Set aside.

Make the Cheese sauce (recipe follows).

Line up seven serving bowls, and place the following ingredients separately into each: cube of butter, sour cream, chives, cooked broccoli and cauliflower, sauteed vegetables, avocado mixture and cheese sauce.

Remove the baked potatoes from oven. Cut the potatoes lengthwise $^3/_4$ way down. Arrange on a large serving platter.

Place all serving bowls and platter of potatoes buffet style on your table. Allow each individual to place desired potato fillings into the center of their potato. Makes 5 servings.

Cheese Sauce

1 tbsp	butter
6 cloves	garlic, pressed
3 tbsp	flour
1 cup	milk
$^1/_2$ cup	white wine
1 tsp	Pickapeppa sauce
$^1/_2$ tsp	garlic salt
$^1/_2$ tsp	salt
$^1/_2$ tsp	white pepper
2 dashes	cayenne pepper
3 cups	cheddar cheese, grated

In a large skillet over medium-high heat, melt butter with garlic. Stir in flour and milk, beating vigorously with a whisk until thickened and there are no lumps. Stir in the remaining ingredients, and cook until heated through and cheese is melted. Pour into a serving bowl and serve with Baked Potato Feast.

Veggie Kabobs

16	small red boiling potatoes
8	small boiling onions
16	medium sized mushrooms
1	red bell pepper
1	medium sized zucchini

Wash and prepare the vegetables. Steam potatoes 15-20 minutes or until just tender. Peel the boiling onions and cut in half. Cut bell pepper into 16 $1^1/_2$ inch pieces. Slice zucchini into 16 $^3/_4$ inch slices. Place all vegetables in a large, shallow dish.

Next, pour Marinade (recipe follows) over vegetables. Stir to coat well. Cover and refrigerate several hours. Toss the vegetables a few times while marinating.

Arrange two of each vegetable on 8 skewers. Grill 15-20 minutes over medium coals, turning frequently. Baste often with the marinade.

Pour remaining marinade in a small serving bowl and serve as a dipping sauce alongside the skewers. Makes 8 servings.

Veggie Kabob Marinade

$^1/_2$ cup	soy sauce	$^1/_2$ cup	Japanese Sake (rice wine)
$^1/_4$ cup	brown sugar		
2 cloves	garlic, pressed	1 tsp	sesame oil
1 tsp	fresh ginger, minced	$^1/_4$ tsp	onion powder
		$^1/_4$ cup	rice vinegar
		$^1/_4$ cup	water

Stir together all ingredients.

Stuffed Green Peppers

6	large green peppers
1 tbsp	butter
1/2 cup	onion, chopped
15 oz	can stewed tomatoes, cut up (including liquid)
1 cup	long grain rice (uncooked)
1 1/4 cups	water
1 tsp	salt
1 tsp	Pickapeppa sauce
1 tsp	chili powder
1/8 tsp	white pepper
1 cup	Monterey Jack cheese, grated
1 cup	walnuts, chopped

Cut tops from green peppers. Scrape inside with a metal spoon, removing seeds and membranes. Chop enough of the tops to make 1/4 cup. Set aside. Cook whole green peppers in boiling water for 5 minutes; invert to drain well.

In a skillet over medium-high heat, sauté onions and chopped green peppers in butter. Add the undrained stewed tomatoes, rice, water, salt, Pickapeppa sauce, chili powder and white pepper. Bring to a boil, then reduce heat. Cover and simmer 20-25 minutes, or until rice is tender and most of the liquid is absorbed. Stir in cheese and nuts.

Stuff the peppers with rice mixture. Place in a 10x6x2 inch baking dish. Cover with foil and bake in a 350° oven for 30-35 minutes. Makes 6 servings.

Savoy Cabbage and Spinch Roll-ups with Mild Curry Cheese Sauce

2 bunches	spinach
1 head	savoy cabbage
2 tbsp	butter
1³/₄ tsp	salt
2 cups	fresh mushrooms, sliced
3 tbsp	flour
1 cup	milk
2 cloves	garlic, pressed
¹/₂ tsp	curry powder
¹/₄ cup	dry sherry
2 cups	Jack cheese, grated
1	egg

Wash and trim spinach. Steam in ¹/₂ cup water until just wilted. Place in a colander under cold running water, until cool. Squeeze as dry as possible, and chop fine. Set aside.

Core cabbage. Remove leaves in whole pieces. With a knife, remove center vein, keeping leaves in one piece. Fill a large saucepan with water and 1 tsp salt. Bring to a boil. Drop in cabbage leaves for approximately 1 minute or until limp. Drain, then pat dry with paper towels. Set aside.

Melt butter in a large skillet over medium high heat. Add mushrooms and ¹/₂ tsp salt. Sauté until mushrooms are tender. Remove the mushrooms to a separate bowl, leaving liquid in pan. Reduce heat to medium. Stir in flour and milk with a whisk and beat vigorously until there are no lumps and sauce begins to thicken. Stir in garlic, curry powder, ¹/₄ tsp salt, and dry sherry until well combined. Add the cheese, stirring constantly until cheese melts. Stir in the sautéed mushrooms. Pour half the sauce into a medium sized bowl. Stir in chopped spinach and egg until well combined.

To assemble: Spread approximately 3-4 tablespoons of spinach mixture evenly over entire surface of each cabbage leaf. Roll up jelly-roll style. (When down to the smaller cabbage leaves, lay two leaves together to form the size of a large one). Place seam side down in a 12x8x2 inch baking dish.

Pour remaining cheese sauce over top of all cabbage rolls. Bake in a 350° oven for 20 minutes. Serve hot.

Makes 8 rolls.

Cabbage Rolls

¹/₄ cup	butter	16 oz	can stewed tomatoes, cut up (reserve 1 cup of the liquid)
2 cups	mushrooms, chopped		
1 cup	celery, sliced	1	egg, slightly beaten
1 cup	onion, chopped	2 cups	cooked rice
¹/₄ tsp	oregano	1 cup	slivered almonds
¹/₄ tsp	marjoram	15 oz	can tomato sauce
¹/₄ tsp	thyme	1 tsp	dried parsley
¹/₈ tsp	sage	9	large green cabbage leaves
2 cups	dry seasoned stuffing mix		

In a large skillet, melt butter. Add mushrooms, celery, onion, oregano, marjoram, ¹/₈ teaspoon of the thyme, and sage. Sauté until vegetables are tender. In a medium sized bowl, stir together the sauteed vegetables with the stuffing mix. Stir in stewed tomatoes, along with ¹/₂ cup of the liquid, egg, rice and slivered almonds. Mix well.

In a small saucepan over medium heat, combine the tomato sauce, remaining ¹/₂ cup of the stewed tomato liquid, parsley, and remaining ¹/₈ teaspoon thyme. Cover and let simmer for 15 minutes.

Remove center vein of cabbage leaves, keeping each leaf in 1 piece. Place leaves in boiling water for about 3 minutes, or until limp. Drain.

Place ¹/₂ cup of stuffing mixture in the center of each leaf; fold envelope style. Place seam side down in 12x8x2 inch baking dish. Pour tomato mixture evenly over top. Bake uncovered in a 350° oven for 1¹/₄ hours, basting once or twice with sauce. Serve warm. Makes 9 servings.

Stuffed Beefsteak Tomatoes

4	beefsteak or extra large tomatoes
1 cup	cauliflower pieces
1 cup	broccoli pieces
¾ cup	red onion, diced
½ cup	mayonnaise
½ tsp	Vege-Sal All Purpose Seasoning
8	large lettuce leafs

Hollow out the center of each tomato. Invert the tomatoes to drain for 20 minutes. Cut tomatoes into quarters to (but not through) the bottom, so each quarter fans out. Set aside.

Place the cauliflower and broccoli in a medium sized saucepan with ¹/₂ cup water. Cook over high heat until water begins to boil. Cover, reduce heat to low, and let vegetables steam for about 10 minutes or until tender-crisp. Strain in a colander, then place under cold running water until vegetables have cooled down. After vegetables have cooled, dice into small pieces.

In a medium sized bowl, stir together the cooled vegetables, onion, mayonnaise, and Vege-Sal All Purpose Seasoning until well combined and vegetables are evenly coated.

Arrange two lettuce leafs on each plate, place the tomato in center, then top each with a scoop of the filling. Chill until ready to serve. Makes 4 servings.

Zucchini Boats

5	medium sized zucchini
1 slice	sourdough bread
2 tbsp	butter
2	small red potatoes, finely diced
2	large mushrooms, finely diced
5	scallions, finely diced
5 cloves	garlic, pressed
$1/2$ tsp	Vege-Sal All Purpose Seasoning
$1/2$ tsp	salt
$1/2$ tsp	garlic salt
$1/4$ tsp	black pepper
$1/4$ tsp	cayenne pepper
$3/4$ cup	Swiss cheese, grated
$3/4$ cup	fresh Parmesan cheese, grated
2 tbsp	olive oil

Cut the zucchini into halves and scoop out the seeds with a spoon. Place zucchini in a medium sized baking pan. Set aside.

Tear the sourdough bread into pieces and place in a blender. Blend just enough to create fresh bread crumbs. Place crumbs in a small bowl. Set aside.

In a medium sized skillet, melt butter. Add the potatoes, mushrooms, scallions, garlic and remaining 5 spices. Lightly sauté over medium-low heat for about 1 minute. Add the Swiss and Parmesan cheese,and bread crumbs. Stir until cheese is thoroughly melted.

Fill each zucchini boat with a generous amount of filling. Brush the tops with olive oil and bake in a 375° oven for 15-20 minutes. Serve hot. Makes 10 boats.

Green and Yellow Squash in Red Sauce

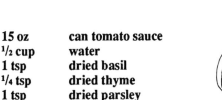

15 oz	**can tomato sauce**
¹/₂ cup	**water**
1 tsp	**dried basil**
¹/₄ tsp	**dried thyme**
1 tsp	**dried parsley**
¹/₄ tsp	**salt**
¹/₈ tsp	**black pepper**
1	**medium size zucchini, sliced (approx. 2 cups)**
1	**medium size yellow squash, sliced (approx. 1¹/₂ cups)**
4 cups	**cooked rice**

In a medium sized saucepan, combine the tomato sauce, water, basil, thyme, parsley, salt and pepper. Bring to a boil over medium heat. Reduce heat to medium low, then stir in the squash. Cover and let simmer 15 minutes, or until squash is tender, stirring occasionally.

Serve over rice. Makes 4 servings.

Zesty Mushroom Sauté

½ cup	butter
2 tsp	garlic powder
8 cups	mushrooms, sliced
2	lemons, juiced
	salt to taste
	pepper to taste

Melt butter in a large saucepan over medium heat. Stir in garlic powder and mushrooms. As the mushrooms cook down, add the lemon juice and continue to stir. Cook the mushrooms until tender but still firm. Season with salt and pepper to taste. Makes 6-8 servings.

Chinese Cuisine

Fresh Green Bean Chop Suey

—M. FALCO—

The following recipe accentuates the Green Bean (our favorite is the Blue Lake variety). It is easy to prepare, pleasing to the eye, and delicious. Depending on your taste, you can add bean sprouts, or any other type vegetable. Just remember, the longest cooking vegetables are put in the pot first.

3.85 oz	package bean threads	6 cups	fresh green beans, diagonally sliced
1 cup	soy sauce	½ cup	carrots, diagonally sliced
1 pinch	cayenne pepper		
¾ cup	water	1 cup	celery stalks, sliced
1 tsp	vegetable oil	7 slices	fresh ginger, ⅛ inch thick
1 tbsp	sesame oil		
1 tbsp	garlic, minced	1 cup	mushrooms, sliced
1 tbsp	fresh ginger, finely chopped	8 oz	can of water chestnuts
		¼ cup	red bell pepper, sliced
1 cup	onion, chopped		

Place the bean threads in a saucepan full of hot tap water. Set aside until cooking is completed. The bean threads will be the last ingredient added, and need to soak at least 20 minutes.

Combine soy sauce, cayenne pepper and water in a separate bowl. Set aside.

Heat both oils in a dutch oven or large saucepan over high heat until hot. Add the garlic, ginger and onions. Sauté until onions become transparent. Then add the soy sauce/water mixture. Bring to a boil.

Add the green beans, carrots, celery and seven slices of ginger root. Reduce heat to medium-high and cook until the beans begin to soften. **DO NOT OVER COOK**. You want the beans to be firm and crunchy. Next, add the mushrooms, water chestnuts and red bell pepper. Cook another 3 minutes. Remove from heat and cover. Remove the ginger slices.

Drain the bean threads. Cut the threads into 2 to 4 inch lengths with scissors. Add threads to the vegetables and mix well.

Serve over chow mein noodles or rice. Makes 6-8 servings.

Szechuan Noodle Salad

1¹/₂ lbs	Whole Wheat Udon Noodles (found in health food stores)
¹/₂ tsp	salt
1 tbsp	vegetable oil
1 cup	peanut oil
1 tbsp	sesame oil
¹/₄ cup	tamari soy sauce
³/₄ tsp	cayenne pepper
¹/₂ tsp	fresh ginger, minced
3 cloves	garlic, pressed
³/₄ cup	scallions, chopped
2 cups	fresh mushrooms, finely chopped
1¹/₂ cups	un-salted peanuts
8 oz	sliced water chestnuts, quartered

Fill a large saucepan with water. Add salt and vegetable oil. Bring to a boil. Add Udon Noodles and cook uncovered, stirring occasionally for 15 minutes, or until noodles are tender. Drain and set aside.

In a blender, add peanut and sesame oil, tamari soy sauce, cayenne pepper, ginger and garlic. Blend until smooth and creamy. Add ¹/₄ cup of the scallions, and blend for a few seconds until onion is chopped fine.

Transfer noodles into a large bowl. Pour on dressing and toss until well coated. Allow noodles to cool to room temperature, tossing occasionally. Gently toss in remaining scallions, mushrooms, peanuts and water chestnuts. Cover and refrigerte for at least an hour before serving, or overnight. Toss once just before serving. Makes 8-10 servings.

Bean Curd in Szechuan Sauce

4 10.5 oz packages, fresh firm tofu
¹/₂ cup	**soy sauce**
¹/₂ cup	**white wine**
4 tbsp	**cornstarch**
¹/₂ cup	**sesame oil**
¹/₂ cup	**rice vinegar**
¹/₃ cup	**brown sugar**
10 cloves	**garlic, pressed**
¹/₂ tsp	**cayenne pepper**
1 tsp	**minced ginger**
1 bunch	**scallions, chopped**
1 cup	**fresh or frozen tiny peas**

Cut tofu into ¹/₂ inch cubes, and set aside in a strainer to remove any liquid.

In a large skillet, stir together the soy sauce, white wine, cornstarch, oil, vinegar, sugar, garlic, cayenne and ginger. Place over medium high heat, stirring constantly, until sauce is bubbly and thickened.

Gently stir the tofu, scallions and peas into the sauce. Continue to cook until heated through. Serve over Stir-Fried Rice or plain rice. Makes 4-6 servings.

Stir-Fry Rice

7 cups	long grain rice, precooked and chilled (before cooking thoroughly rinse rice to remove starch)
2 tbsp	sesame oil
4 tbsp	peanut oil
2 cloves	garlic, minced
3 tsp	fresh ginger, minced
1	medium sized carrot, diced
2 cups	mushrooms, chopped
1 tbsp	soy sauce
4	eggs, slightly beaten
10 oz	package frozen peas
1 tbsp	salt
3 tbsp	Hoisin sauce
2 cups	bean sprouts
8 oz	can bamboo shoots, thinly sliced
8 oz	can water chestnuts, chopped
2 bunches	scallions, finely chopped

Flake the rice so that the grains don't stick together. Set aside.

In a large saucepan, heat the sesame and peanut oil over medium-high until hot. Add the garlic and ginger. Stir-fry for 30 seconds. Add carrots and mushrooms, stir-frying for 1 minute, then add the soy sauce and continue stirring for 30 seconds. Strain the cooked vegetables over a bowl and let them drain well. Return the liquid from drained vegetables to pan.

Add the rice and cook until heated through without browning. Working quickly, make a well in the center of the rice. Add the eggs, stirring constantly. When eggs have a soft-scrambled consistency, start incorporating the rice, stirring in a circular motion until well blended.

Add the peas and salt. Stir in the Hosin sauce, tossing the rice many times to blend evenly. Stir in the bean sprouts, bamboo shoots, waterchestnuts, cooked mushrooms and carrots. Stir and toss about 1 minute. Add the scallions, toss again, and serve immediately. Makes 8-12 servings.

Vegetable Tempura

12	broccoli flowerets	4¹/₂ cups	water
2	carrots	3²/₃ cups	flour
1	zucchini	3 tsp	salt
2	onions	¹/₃ tsp	pepper
1	sweet potato	¹/₃ tsp	white pepper
¹/₂ head	cauliflower	3 tbsp	vegetable oil
12	mushrooms	4	eggs, slightly beaten

Wash and prepare the vegetables. Cut 12 flowerets from broccoli stalks. Peel and quarter carrots into 12 pieces cut into 3-4 inch lengths. Quarter zucchini into 12 pieces and cut into 3-4 inch lengths. Slice onions into 12 ¹/₄ inch thick slices. Slice sweet potato into 12 ¹/₄ inch thick slices. Cut cauliflower into 12 bite-size pieces. Thoroughly scrub mushrooms, and set all vegetables aside until called for.

Make tempura batter. In a large mixing bowl, stir together flour, salt, pepper, white pepper, oil, eggs, and water. Stir until thoroughly mixed.

In a deep fryer or large saucepan, heat oil to approximately 350-375° F. Dip vegetables a few at a time in tempura batter to lightly coat, then drop into the hot oil. Fry vegetables until the batter turns a golden brown. Remove with a slotted metal spoon, and place on a plate lined with paper towel. Continue this procedure until all the vegetables are used.

Arrange all tempura vegetables on a large serving platter or on individual plates. Serve with Tempura Dipping Sauce (recipe follows) on the side. Serve immediately. Makes 4-6 servings.

Tempura Dipping Sauce

³/₄ cup	soy sauce
2 tbsp	sugar
2 tbsp	brown sugar
¹/₄ cup	rice vinegar
¹/₂ tsp	ground ginger
1¹/₂ cups	water

Stir together soy sauce, sugar, brown sugar, rice vinegar, ginger and water. Place into individual serving cups.

Hot and Sour Soup

.7 oz	package Dried Forest Mushrooms
2 cups	button mushrooms, sliced thick
1 tbsp	peanut oil
1 tbsp	ginger, minced
1 tsp	garlic, minced
8 oz	can bamboo shoots, thinly sliced
1 cup	light soy sauce
4 cups	water
7 tbsp	red wine vinegar (or to taste)
2 tbsp	cornstarch
3 tbsp	water
2 14.2 oz	pads fresh firm tofu, cut into ½ inch cubes
2	eggs, lightly beaten
1 tbsp	sesame oil
2 tsp	ground white pepper
2 tbsp	chopped scallions, for garnish

Place dried black mushrooms in a small bowl. Cover with boiling water and let stand for 15 minutes. Drain. Cut off and discard mushroom stems. Slice thin and set aside.

Add peanut oil in a dutch oven pan and place on medium-high heat. When the oil is hot, stir in the ginger and garlic. Add both kinds of mushrooms, and the bamboo shoots. Stir quickly for approximately 1 minute. Next, add the soy sauce, water and vinegar, while continuing to stir.

In a small cup, mix the cornstarch with 3 tablespoons of water. Stir into the simmering broth. When slightly thickened, add the tofu cubes. Bring to a boil, then turn off the heat. (Let the broth cool a bit so the eggs do not overcook when they are added.)

Add the sesame oil and pepper. Stir to blend. Pour the soup into a hot soup tureen. Gradually add the eggs in a thin stream, stirring in a circular motion. Sprinkle with scallions. Serve immediately. Makes 6-8 servings.

Mexican Cuisine

Burrito Feast

16 oz	can vegetarian refried beans
2 tsp	Pickapeppa sauce
1/4 tsp +	
1/3 tsp	salt
1/4 tsp	hot pepper sauce
1/4 tsp	white pepper
1/4 tsp	black pepper
1/4 tsp	cayenne pepper
2 tbsp	butter
14.2 oz	package firm tofu, cut into 1/2 inch cubes
1/2 tsp	Vege-Sal All Purpose Seasoning
3	medium-large ripe avocados
2 tbsp	mayonnaise
2 cups	cheddar cheese, grated
2	large tomatoes, diced
1/2 cup	red onion, chopped
1/2 cup	white onion, chopped
1 cup	sour cream
10	large flour or corn tortillas

In a medium saucepan over medium heat, stir together the refried beans, 1 teaspoon of the Pickapeppa sauce, 1/4 teaspoon of the salt, hot pepper sauce, white and black peppers and cayenne pepper. Turn the heat to low and simmer while preparing the remaining ingredients.

Melt butter in a medium sized skillet. Add tofu cubes and Vege-Sal All Purpose Seasoning. Stir gently until heated through. Drain and set aside.

In a small mixing bowl, blend the avocados, mayonnaise, remaining 1 teaspoon Pickapeppa sauce and $^1/_3$ teaspoon salt, with an electric mixer until smooth.

Wrap the tortillas in foil and place in a 350° oven for 10-15 minutes or until hot.

Remove the simmering beans from heat. Line up seven serving bowls and place the following ingredients separately in each: bean mixture, tofu cubes, avocado mixture, grated cheddar cheese, diced tomatoes, red and white onions combined, and sour cream.

Remove the heated tortillas from oven and place on a serving plate.

Arrange all the serving bowls and plate of hot tortillas on your table buffet style. Have each person add the desired amount of burrito fillings into the center of their tortilla, and roll up burrito style. Do not over stuff burritos or you will have trouble rolling them up. Devour! Makes 10 burritos.

Vegetarian Tacos

2 tbsp	butter
²/₃ cup	onion, chopped
16 oz	can stewed tomatoes, cut up (reserve the liquid)
1 cup	water
1 cup	long grain rice
1 tbsp	brown sugar
1 tbsp	Pickapeppa sauce
1 tsp	salt
1 tsp	chili powder
¹/₈ tsp	hot pepper sauce
8-10	taco shells
1 cup	sour cream
1¹/₂ cups	cheddar cheese, grated
1 cup	ripe olives, sliced
1¹/₂ cups	lettuce, shredded
1 cup	salsa (see recipe page 18 or use your favorite brand)

Make Spanish rice by melting butter in a large saucepan over medium-high heat. Add onion and cook until tender. Stir in undrained tomatoes, water, rice, brown sugar, Pickapeppa sauce, salt, chili powder and hot pepper sauce. Cover and simmer for approximately 30 minutes or until rice is done and liquid is absorbed.

Scoop a large spoonful of rice into the bottom of taco shell. Spread about a tablespoon of sour cream on top of the rice. Layer with cheese, olives and lettuce. Drizzle approximately 2 tablespoons of salsa over the top. Makes 8-10 servings.

Mexican Tofu Tostada with Hot and Spicy Sour Cream Dressing

2 16 oz	cans refried beans, vegetarian
1 tsp	salt
2 tbsp	butter
14.2 oz	package fresh firm tofu, cut into ½ inch cubes
1 tsp	Vege-Sal All Purpose Seasoning
3 cups	cheddar cheese, grated
1 head	green leaf lettuce, thinly sliced
2	ripe avocados, diced
3	medium sized tomatoes, chopped
1 cup	red onion, chopped

In a medium sized saucepan, heat the refried beans and salt. Spread evenly over four dinner plates.

Melt butter in a medium sized skillet over medium heat. Add tofu and Vege-Sal All Purpose Seasoning. Stir gently until tofu is heated through. Divide and spread the tofu evenly over beans.

Evenly layer the lettuce, cheese, avocado, tomatoes and onions over beans and tofu. Drizzle desired amount of Hot and Spicy Sour Cream Dressing (recipe follows) over top. Makes 4 servings.

Hot and Spicy Sour Cream Dressing

²/₃ cup	mayonnaise
¹/₃ cup	sour cream
2 tsp	Pickapeppa sauce
¹/₂ tsp	white pepper
¹/₂ tsp	garlic salt
¹/₄ tsp	hot pepper sauce
1	very small jalapeño pepper

Place all ingredients in a blender. Blend until smooth. Pour evenly over tostadas.

Jack and Olive Enchiladas

1 lb	Monterey Jack cheese, grated (approx. 4 cups)
8 oz	can ripe olives, chopped (approx. 1¹/₂ cups)
1 cup	enchilada sauce
1 cup	sour cream
8	corn tortillas
2 tbsp	vegetable oil

In a large skillet over medium-high heat, heat oil until hot. Fry tortillas in hot oil for a few seconds on each side, until limp. (Add a little extra oil if needed.) Drain tortillas on spread out paper towels. Sprinkle a generous amount of cheese and olives in middle of each tortilla. Roll up and place seam side down in a 12x8x2 inch baking dish.

In a bowl, combine the sour cream and enchilada sauce. Pour evenly over the top of enchiladas. Top with any remaining olives and cheese. Bake in a 350° oven for 25 minutes, or until bubbly and cheese is melted. Makes 8 enchiladas.

Italian Cuisine

Mini Vegetarian Pizza's

Using the sourdough English muffins in this recipe is not only extremely convenient, but absolutely delicious as well. We're hooked!

12	sourdough English muffins	1/2 tsp	salt
		1/2 tsp	marjoram
24	medium slices Mozzarella cheese	1/2 tsp	thyme
		1/2 tsp	oregano
		1/4 tsp	black pepper
24	medium slices tomato	1/4 tsp	cayenne pepper
		1	medium yellow onion, chopped
1/4 cup + 2 tbsp	butter	3	large mushrooms, chopped
1/4 cup	olive oil		
8-10 cloves	garlic	1/2	green pepper, chopped
1 1/2 tsp	garlic salt	8 oz	cheddar cheese, grated
16 oz	can tomato sauce	2.5 oz	Parmesan cheese, grated
12 oz	can tomato paste		
1/3 cup	dry red wine	4 1/2 oz	can sliced ripe olives
2	bay leaves		

Melt 1/4 cup butter in a saucepan and set aside. In a blender, add olive oil, 4-5 cloves garlic, and 1 teaspoon of the garlic salt. Pour melted butter in and blend thoroughly. Transfer mixture back into saucepan and set aside.

Line 2 cookie sheets with foil. Open English muffins and arrange on sheets. Generously brush each English muffin with the butter, oil and garlic mixture. Set aside.

In a medium saucepan, combine tomato sauce, tomato paste, wine, bay leaves, the remaining 4-5 garlic cloves (this time pressed), the remaining $1/2$ teaspoon garlic salt, and the rest of the spices. Simmer the sauce while sauteing the vegetables.

In a small skillet, melt 2 tablespoons butter. Add onion, mushrooms and green peppers. Sauté lightly for 1-2 minutes. Set aside. Remove simmering red sauce from heat and also set aside.

In a small bowl, stir together the cheddar and Parmesan cheeses, and olives. Set aside.

To each buttered muffin half, layer in order, one slice Mozzarella cheese, a large spoonful of red sauce, one slice tomato and one small spoonful sauteed vegetables. On the tops of each, evenly sprinkle on the cheese and olive mixture.

Bake in a 350° oven for 10-15 minutes. Serve hot. Makes 24 mini pizzas.

Bill's Spaghetti Blast

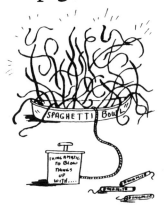

Most husbands don't teach wives to cook, but this bachelor had a few recipes of his own when we met.

32 oz	jar Paul Newman's Spaghetti Sauce (Sockarooni)
28 oz	can Contadina Crushed Tomatoes in Tomato Purée
3 6 oz	cans Contadina Italian Paste
10-12	garlic cloves, pressed
1	medium sized zucchini, chopped
1	medium sized onion, chopped
4	medium sized mushrooms, chopped
1¼ cups	dry red wine
½ tsp	ground Mexican oregano
½ tsp	Mexican oregano leaves
1 tsp	salt
½ tsp	black pepper
3	bay leaves
½ tsp	cayenne pepper
1 tsp	garlic salt
1 tsp	thyme
1 tsp	marjoram
16 oz	package Ronzoni spaghetti
5 oz	fresh Parmesan cheese, grated

In a large saucepan over medium-high heat, add spaghetti sauce, crushed tomatoes, tomato paste and garlic. Cook, stirring constantly, until sauce begins to boil. Reduce heat to medium-low. Stir in all the remaining ingredients except for Ronzoni spaghetti and Parmesan cheese. Cover and let simmer 45 minutes, stirring occasionally.

Cook the Ronzoni spaghetti according to package directions. Place the spaghetti sauce, Ronzoni spaghetti and cheese in individual serving bowls. Serve immediately. (Great with garlic lover's bread, see page 136.) Makes 10 servings.

Eggplant Parmigiana

16 oz	can tomato sauce
6 oz	can tomato paste
2 cloves	garlic, pressed
²/₃ cup	Cabernet Sauvignon wine (or your favorite dry red wine)
¹/₈ tsp	sage
¹/₈ tsp	ground oregano
¹/₄ tsp	basil
¹/₄ tsp	ground thyme
¹/₈ tsp	cayenne pepper
1 tsp	salt
1	medium sized eggplant
2 tsp	dried parsley
1 cup	French bread crumbs (fine)
2	eggs
6 tbsp	butter
1 lb	Mozzarella cheese, thinly sliced
1 cup	fresh Parmesan cheese, grated

In a medium saucepan, combine tomato sauce, tomato paste, garlic, wine, sage, oregano, basil, thyme, cayenne pepper and salt. Simmer for 30 minutes.

Wash, dry, and cut the eggplant into ¹/₄ inch slices. Place slices in a bowl and cover with cold water. Let stand for 5 minutes. Drain the slices thoroughly and dry them on spread out paper towels.

Combine the parsley and French bread crumbs. Spread evenly on a plate. In a small bowl, slightly beat eggs. Dip each slice of eggplant into egg, then roll in bread crumbs covering each slice completely. Sauté in 1 tablespoon butter for approx. 1¹/₂ minutes on each side, or until golden brown. Repeat this procedure using extra butter as needed until all eggplant slices are cooked.

Put a layer of eggplant in the bottom of a casserole dish. Sprinkle with half of the Parmesan cheese. Cover with half of the red sauce and a layer of mozzarella cheese. Repeat a second time in this order, using all the ingredients (with the exception of several slices of mozzarella cheese). Finish with a layer of eggplant. Cover with remaining slices of mozzarella cheese. Bake the casserole in a 350° oven for about 20 minutes, or until the cheese turns slightly brown. Serve very hot. Makes 8 servings.

Spinach Lasagna

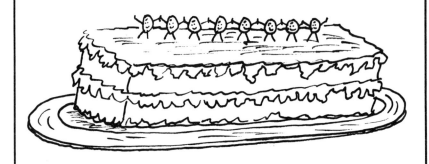

23 oz	can tomato sauce
6 oz	can tomato paste
3 cloves	garlic, pressed
¹/₂ tsp	ground thyme
¹/₄ tsp	sage
¹/₂ tsp	ground oregano
1 tsp	basil
¹/₂ tsp	salt
¹/₂ tsp	white pepper
¹/₄ cup	Cabernet Sauvignon wine (or your favorite dry red wine)
¹/₂ cup	ripe olives, sliced
1 cup	mushrooms, sliced
¹/₄ cup	onion, diced
2	bunches spinach, washed and trimmed
8 oz	small curd cottage cheese (1 cup)
8 oz	Ricotta cheese (1 cup)
1	egg
¹/₂ tsp	pesto paste (see recipe page 20)
9	lasagna noodles
2 lbs.	Mozzarella cheese, sliced

In a medium sized saucepan, stir together the tomato sauce, tomato paste, garlic, thyme, sage, oregano, basil, salt, pepper and wine. Add the olives, mushrooms, and onions. Place on medium high heat until sauce comes to a boil. Reduce heat to low, cover, and simmer 30 minutes, stirring occasionally.

Place spinach in a large saucepan with ¹/₂ cup water. Bring to a boil over high heat, then reduce to low. Cover saucepan with lid and steam spinach until just wilted. Place in a colander under cold running water until spinach has cooled down. Squeeze spinach as dry as possible, then on a cutting board finely chop.

In a small mixing bowl, blend the cottage cheese, Ricotta cheese, egg and pesto paste until well blended. Stir in the chopped spinach.

In a large saucepan, cook the lasagna noodles as directed on package.

To assemble, spoon a small amount of red sauce over bottom of 12x8x2 inch casserole dish. Top with three strips cooked lasagna. Spread with half of the cheese filling, cover with generous amount of red sauce, then a layer of mozzarella cheese. Repeat layers, ending with mozzarella cheese. Place last three strips of lasagna on top, spread a small amount of red sauce over noodles, then a layer of mozzarella cheese.

Bake in a 350° oven for 30 minutes, or until thoroughly heated and cheese is melted. Let stand 5-10 minutes to set layers. Makes 8 servings.

Two Way Fettucine

FETTUCIN'I

#1 Fettucine with Traditional Sauce

12 oz	**package fettucine noodles**
¹⁄₃ cup	**butter**
4 tbsp	**flour**
2 cups	**milk**
1 tsp	**salt**
5 oz	**Parmesan cheese, grated**
1 pint	**sour cream**

Prepare fettucine noodles according to package directions.

In a large skillet over medium-high heat, melt butter. With a whisk, stir in flour and milk, beating vigorously until creamy and there are no lumps. Stirring constantly, add the salt and cheese. Continue cooking until sauce thickens and cheese is melted. Stir in the sour cream. Heat through, but do not boil.

Pour sauce over cooked fettucine noodles; gently toss until all noodles are evenly coated. Or, for a spicier fettucine sauce, try Fettucine Sauce of the 90's (recipe follows). Serve immediately. 4 servings.

#2 Fettucine Sauce of the 90's

¹/₃ cup	butter
5 cloves	garlic, pressed
¹/₂ cup	onions, diced
4 tbsp	flour
1 cup	milk
¹/₂ cup	heavy or whipping cream
¹/₂ cup	white wine
1 tsp	salt
¹/₂ tsp	garlic salt
¹/₂ tsp	white pepper
1 tsp	thyme
5 oz	Parmesan cheese, grated

In a large skillet over medium-high heat, melt butter. Add the garlic and onions; sauté until tender. With a whisk, stir in flour and milk. Beat vigorously until creamy and there are no lumps. Stirring constantly, add the cream, wine, salt, garlic salt, pepper, thyme and cheese. Continue cooking until sauce thickens and cheese is melted.

Pour sauce over cooked fettucine noodles; gently toss until all noodles are evenly coated. Makes 4 servings.

Angel Hair Pasta
with Herbs and Spices

10 oz	angel hair pasta
½ cup	butter
2 tbsp	olive oil
1 tsp	dried basil
1 tsp	dried oregano
1 tsp	salt
½ tsp	pepper
2 tbsp	dried parsley flakes
6 cloves	garlic, pressed
½ tsp	garlic salt

Cook pasta according to package directions. Place into a medium sized serving bowl.

In a medium sized skillet, over medium-high heat, melt butter. Add all the remaining ingredients. Cook for one minute, stirring occasionally, until very hot. Pour over angel hair pasta, and gently toss to evenly coat. Makes 4 servings.

Thanksgiving the Vegetarian Way

Menu

We thought the biggest test for our vegetarian lifestyle would be during Thanksgiving. Raiding the icebox at 2:00 a.m. for that cold turkey sandwich sounded like too much to give up. It's not. A stuffing and cranberry sandwich with a little mayo will do the trick, and the turkey can play the fiddle at your feast!

Appetizers

    Artichoke Parmesan Dip (see page 9)

    The Olive and Cheese Act (see page 12)

The Feast

    Vegetable Casserole

    Whipped Potatoes with Sliced Mushroom Gravy

    Honey Flavored Yams in Orange halves

    Ten Ingredient Salad with Herb Dressing (see page 21)

    Onion, Mushroom Stuffing

    Herb Biscuits

    Fresh Cran-Raspberry Relish

    Cranberry Surprise Molded Salad

Desserts

    Claire's Carrot Cake

    T.J.'s Pumpkin Pie with Fresh Whipped Cream

    Dessert Coffee (see page 134)

    Serves 8-10 well!

Vegetable Casserole

3	large slices sourdough bread, torn into small bite-sized pieces
4 cups	fresh whole baby carrots, peeled
2 cups	fresh peas, cut in half
2 cups	fresh string beans, cut into one inch lengths
8 oz	Romano Cheese, grated
$1/2$ cup	boiling water
$1/2$ cup	butter
2 tbsp	fresh lemon juice
1	vegetable bouillon cube
2 tsp	Lemon and Pepper Seasoning Salt
1 tsp	salt
$1/2$ tsp	garlic salt

Steam carrots, peas and string beans together, adding carrots to steamer first, because they take longer to cook. Drain and set aside in a large mixing bowl.

In a small saucepan, melt butter. Add boiling water and vegetable bouillon cube. Stir until cube dissolves. Stir in the lemon juice and spices, and pour over vegetables.

Add the sourdough bread pieces and the cheese to the veggies. Lightly toss to mix well.

Gently scoop mixture into a covered casserole dish and bake in a 350° oven for 25-30 minutes.

Whipped Potatoes with Sliced Mushroom Gravy

Whipped Potatoes

10	medium russet potatoes
³/₄ cup	milk
¹/₄ cup	butter, softened
1¹/₂ tsp	salt

In two large saucepans boil potatoes until fork tender. Let cool. Cut potatoes into fourths and place in a large mixing bowl. Add milk, butter and salt. Beat on medium speed with an electric mixer until potatoes are smooth and creamy. Place in an oven proof dish, cover with foil and set aside. Reheat potatoes in a 350° oven for 20-30 minutes before serving.

Sliced Mushroom Gravy

1 cup	red wine
1¹/₂ cups	half and half
2 cups	milk
3 cups	mushrooms, sliced (including stems)
1	medium onion, chopped
¹/₄ cup	butter
¹/₃ cup + 1 tbsp	flour
5 cloves	garlic, pressed
1¹/₂ tsp	salt
¹/₂ tsp	garlic salt
¹/₂ tsp	white pepper
¹/₄ tsp	black pepper
¹/₄ tsp	onion powder
1 pinch	cayenne pepper

In a large skillet, melt butter on medium heat. Add wine and flour, stirring constantly until flour is smooth and there are no lumps. Stir in half and half, milk, garlic and spices. Increase heat a little and let come to a slow boil. Continue to stir until gravy thickens, and then reduce heat to simmer. Gently stir in mushrooms and onions, slowly cook for another minute and then set aside.

Note: The gravy will need to be re-heated before serving. Adding the mushrooms and onions last will keep them from over cooking and turning too soft. Also, people tend to use a lot of gravy on their food. You may find it necessary to double this recipe.

Honey Flavored Yams in Orange Halves

8	medium yams
10	oranges halved, with the juice squeezed out
¼ cup	honey
¼ cup	butter, softened
½ cup	orange juice
½ tsp	cinnamon
	cinnamon to taste

Boil yams in a large saucepan until fork-tender. Let cool. Peel yams, cut into medium sized pieces, and place in a large mixing bowl. Add honey, butter, orange juice and ½ tsp cinnamon. Mix with an electric mixer on medium speed until yams are smooth and creamy.

Spoon a generous amount of yams into each of the 20 orange halves. Sprinkle very lightly with additional cinnamon. Place filled orange halves on an aluminum foiled cookie sheet, cover and set aside. Heat in a 350° oven for 15-20 minutes before serving.

Onion Mushroom Stuffing

1 16 oz.	loaf French bread, cut into bite-sized cubes
6	slices whole wheat bread, cut into bite-sized cubes
1	medium onion, chopped
3	stalks celery, chopped (including leaves)
1½ cups	mushrooms, chopped
½ cup	butter
1 cup	white wine
3 cups	boiling water
5 cloves	garlic, pressed
1 tsp	salt
1 tsp	sage
1 tsp	Vege-Sal All Purpose Seasoning
½ tsp	thyme
½ tsp	marjoram
½ tsp	pepper

In a large saucepan, melt butter. Add onion, celery, mushrooms, garlic and spices. Sauté for about 1 minute. Stir in the wine and water, and turn off heat. Pour in the French and whole wheat bread cubes, and toss well to coat. Pour mixture into a 13x9x2 inch baking pan. Heat for 30 minutes in a 350° oven when ready to serve.

Herb Biscuits

3¹/₂ cups	pre-sifted flour (regular or whole wheat)
³/₄ cup	butter, softened
6 tsp	double acting baking powder
¹/₂ cup	vegetable oil
1¹/₂ cups	milk
2 tsp	salt
1¹/₂ tbsp	dried parsley flakes
1 tsp	sage
1 tsp	onion powder
1 tsp	spike

In a large mixing bowl, combine flour, baking powder, herbs and spices. Add butter, milk and vegetable oil, and beat with an electric mixer until smooth.

Pre-heat oven to 375°. On an un-greased cookie sheet, drop tablespoon-sized balls of the dough. Bake for 10-12 minutes, or until tops are golden brown.

Makes 24 biscuits.

Cran-Raspberry Relish

24 oz	fresh cranberries
3 cups	fresh raspberries
2 cups	water
1 cup	sugar
½ cup	honey

In a medium saucepan, add water and sugar, and bring to a boil. Stir in honey, cranberries and raspberries. Lower heat a little, but continue to boil, stirring occasionally for 10-12 minutes. Remove from heat and let cool several hours before serving.

Cranberry Surprise Molded Salad

1 6 oz	box black cherry flavored Jell-o
2 cups	boiling water
2 16 oz	cans whole berry cranberries
1 cup	celery, diced
1 cup	walnuts, chopped
2 cups	sour cream
several	green lettuce leaves

Dissolve Jell-o in hot water. Chill until thick but not firm. Stir in cranberries, celery and walnuts. Gently fold in sour cream. Pour into a salad mold and chill 4-5 hours.

Arrange lettuce leaves on a serving platter. Place salad mold into a bowl of hot water up to the rim, for about 30 seconds. This will loosen the salad. Turn the salad onto the arranged lettuce leaves, chill and serve when ready.

Claire's Carrot Cake

2 cups	sugar
1½ cups	vegetable oil
3 cups	unsifted flour
6	extra large eggs
2 tsp	baking powder
2 tsp	baking soda
2 tsp	cinnamon
½ tsp	salt
2 cups	grated carrots
¾ cup	raisins
20	maraschino cherries, cut into small pieces
2 cups	walnuts

In a large mixing bowl, combine sugar, oil, flour, eggs, baking powder, baking soda, cinnamon and salt. Stir in carrots, raisins, cherries and walnuts. Mix well. Pour mixture into a well-greased 13x9x2 inch pan and bake in a 350° oven for one hour, or until a toothpick inserted in the middle comes out clean. Frost with Cream Cheese Frosting below.

Cream Cheese Frosting

3 8 oz	packages cream cheese
½ cup	sugar
1 tsp	vanilla extract
½ tsp	orange extract

Beat all ingredients together in a medium sized mixing bowl with an electric mixer until smooth. Spread evenly over cooled carrot cake. Keep refrigerated before and after serving.

Makes 12-16 servings.

T.J.'s Pumpkin Pie with Fresh Whipped Cream

This pie makes 6 servings. Depending on your number of guests, you may wish to make a second pie.

1 9 inch	pre-made graham cracker pie crust
3	eggs
16 oz can	pumpkin
1 cup	evaporated milk
½ cup	sugar
½ cup	clover honey
1 tsp	vanilla
1¼ tsp	ground cinnamon
½ tsp	ground ginger
⅓ tsp	ground nutmeg
¼ tsp	ground cloves
¼ tsp	salt

Pre-heat oven to 375°.

Combine all ingredients together in a medium sized mixing bowl, and beat with an elecrtic mixer until well combined.

Pour filling into pie crust. Place on a cookie sheet in case filling overflows. Bake 45 minutes until filling is set and knife inserted 1 inch from edge comes out clean. Refrigerate. Serve with fresh whipped cream below.

Fresh Whipped Cream

1 cup	heavy or whipping cream
2 tbsp	powdered sugar
1 tsp	vanilla
½ tsp	cinnamon

With an electric mixer, beat all ingredients together until whipping cream holds its shape. Top each pumpkin pie slice with a large spoonful.

Makes 2 cups.

Juices, Smoothies & Beverages

Fresh Squeezed Pineapple Grapefruit Juice Over Pineapple Grapefruit Cubes

Freezing juice into cubes allows you to enjoy glasses of ice cold juice, without the dilution of ice. The result is an extra rich, extra smooth drink, delicious to the last drop.

3   large pineapples
15   grapefruits

Juice pineapples and grapefruits. Combine equal amounts of each juice into two large pitchers. Stir well.

With one of the pitchers of juice, fill 3-4 ice cube trays. Refrigerate the other pitcher of juice.

When cubes are frozen, add 4-6 to each glass of juice served. Makes 3-4 dozen ice cubes, and 1 pitcher of juice.

Tracy's Tropical Smoothie

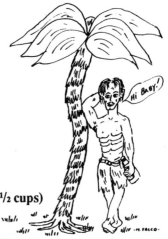

3	oranges, juiced (approx. 1½ cups)
8	whole dates, pitted
1	banana
1 cup	fresh or frozen strawberries
½	papaya, seeded and peeled
12	ice cubes

Pour the orange juice and dates into a blender and blend for one minute. Add the banana, strawberries and papaya. Blend until well combined and creamy. Add 12 ice cubes and blend until all the ice is finely crushed.

Pour into 4 medium sized glasses. Serve immediately. Makes 4 servings.

Pineapple-Banana Smoothie

1 cup	fresh orange juice
10	whole dates, pitted
2 cups	fresh pineapple chunks
2	bananas
12	ice cubes

Add orange juice and dates into blender and blend until dates are chopped fine. Add remaining fruit and blend until smooth. Add ice cubes and blend until ice is finely crushed. Serve immediately. Makes 4 servings.

Red Velvet Smoothie

This drink will remind you of an exotic thick shake. Using the frozen fruit results in this drink's thickness. Great on a hot day.

2½ cups	fresh orange juice
10	whole dates, pitted
1 cup	frozen raspberries
2 cups	frozen whole strawberries

Add orange juice and dates into blender and blend until dates are chopped fine. Add remaining fruit and blend until smooth. Serve immediately. Makes 4 servings.

Strawberry-Banana Smoothie

Children especially love this smoothie because it reminds them of a thick milk shake. Dates are a great natural sweetener.

2¼ cups	fresh orange juice
10	whole dates, pitted
2 cups	frozen whole strawberries
1	large banana

Add orange juice and dates into blender and blend until dates are chopped fine. Add remaining fruit and blend until smooth and creamy. Serve immediately. Makes 4 servings.

Kiwi-Lime Slushie

2	medium sized limes, juiced (approx. ½ cup)
1 cup	water
3	kiwi fruits, peeled
½ cup	honey
18	ice cubes

In a blender, add lime juice, water, 2 kiwi fruits and the honey. Blend well. Add the ice cubes to blender a few at a time, and blend until juice is the consistency of a slushie, but still easy to pour. Pour equal amounts into 4 medium sized glasses. Garnish with a couple slices of kiwi on rim of each glass. Makes 4 servings.

Lemo-Tom Juice

13	tomatoes
4	lemons
2 tbsp	Lemon & Pepper Seasoning
1 tsp	Salt

Cut tomatoes into pieces approximately 3 inches long. Peel lemons, then cut into quarters.

Run all vegetables through juicer, using the juicer screen. Pour juice into a medium sized pitcher. Stir in Lemon & Pepper seasoning and serve. Store in the refrigerator, and stir just before serving. Makes 4 servings.

Spiced Iced Tea

10 cups	water
1	orange
30	whole cloves
2	cinnamon sticks
6	individual tea bags
¼ cup	honey
18	ice cubes

Pour 10 cups water into a large sauce pan. Poke cloves evenly around orange. Add the orange, cinnamon sticks and tea bags to water. Bring to a boil over high heat. Cover saucepan and reduce heat to low. Simmer for 30 minutes.

Remove the tea bags, orange full of cloves, and cinnamon sticks. Stir in honey, and approximately 18 ice cubes to cool down tea. Pour into a large glass jar or pitcher and refrigerate. Serve over a glass filled with ice cubes. Makes 8-10 servings.

Iced Banana Coffee

In this recipe you can use your favorite brand of coffee. We prefer a combination of decaf Colombian and decaf Vanilla Nut cream.

³/₄ cup	ground coffee
10 cups	water
1 cup	half and half
2	bananas
56	ice cubes
6 tbsp	honey

In an automatic drip coffee maker (10 cup capacity) make coffee. Once brewed, remove from burner and let cool until room temperature.

In a blender, mix half and half, bananas and 8 ice cubes until thick and creamy.

Spoon 1 tablespoon honey into each tall ice tea glass. Add coffee until half way filled, stir well. Drop about 8 ice cubes into each coffee, leaving a space of about 1¹/₂ inches from the top. Pour banana cream over the top, leaving the layers separated. Serve immediately with a long stirring stick or straw. Makes 6 servings.

Extra Rich and Creamy
Decaf Dessert Coffee

What a treat after a meal, especially if you're too full for dessert, but still feel like something sweet.

10 cups	**water**
¹/₂ cup	**fresh ground decaf Colombian coffee**
2 tbsp	**fresh ground decaf Espresso**
2	**medium sized cinnamon sticks**
10 tbsp	**honey**
2¹/₂ cups	**half and half**
1 cup	**freshly whipped cream**
	ground cinnamon to taste

Add water to automatic drip coffee maker. Put coffee and espresso in the filter, and place the cinnamon sticks at the bottom of the coffee pot. Brew coffee and let sit on burner for 5 minutes.

Pour coffee into mugs and add 1 tablespoon honey, and ¹/₄ cup half and half. Stir well. top each with one heaping tablespoon of whip cream, then sprinkle lightly with cinnamon. Serve immediately. Makes 10 cups.

Breads, Muffins &
Other Baked Yummies

Garlic Lovers Bread

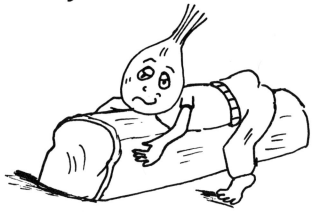

16 oz	loaf french bread
½ cup	butter
⅓ cup	extra virgin olive oil
15 cloves	garlic, pressed (or less, if desired)
1 tbsp	garlic salt
5 oz	fresh Parmesan cheese, grated

Melt butter in a small saucepan over medium-low heat. Pour into a blender along with olive oil, garlic and garlic salt. Blend well.

Cut the french bread into 18 slices, cutting to (but not through) the bottom of the crust. Generously brush each slice of bread with the garlic butter mixture, then sprinkle heavily with Parmesan cheese, pushing some of the cheese down between the slices.

Wrap the bread in foil, and heat in a 350° oven for 12-15 minutes, or until cheese is melted and hot. Makes 9-15 servings.

Corny Corn Bread

1½ cups	flour
1½ cups	yellow corn meal
1 tsp	baking soda
1 tsp	double-acting baking powder
1 tsp	salt
⅓ cup	honey
⅓ cup	vegetable oil
1	egg
2 cups	buttermilk
2 cups	whole-kernel fresh or frozen corn

Stir all ingredients together until well blended. Pour into a well-greased 14x9x2 inch baking pan. Place in a 350° oven for 30 minutes, or until toothpick inserted comes out clean. Cool, cut into squares and serve with Honey Butter (recipe follows). Makes 24 squares.

Honey Butter

½ cup	butter
⅓ cup	honey

In a small mixing bowl, whip butter and honey until light and fluffy.

Zucchini Spice Bread

1 cup	brown sugar
1/2 cup	sugar
3/4 cup	vegetable oil
3	eggs
1/2 tsp	vanilla
2 cups	zucchini, shredded (including peel)
1 cup	red delicious apple, shredded (including peel)
2 1/4 cups	flour
1 1/2 tsp	baking soda
3/4 tsp	salt
1/2 tsp	baking powder
1 tsp	cinnamon
1/4 tsp	ground nutmeg
1/8 tsp	ground cloves
1 cup	raisins
1 cup	chopped walnuts

Beat sugars and oil until well mixed. Add eggs and vanilla, and beat briefly, just enough to mix. Stir in shredded zucchini and apple.

In a separate bowl, sift flour, baking soda, salt, baking powder, cinnamon, nutmeg and cloves. Stir flour mixture into batter until well blended. Add raisins and walnuts. Stir well.

Pour batter into two well-greased medium sized loaf pans. Bake in a 350° oven for 45-50 minutes or until wooden pick inserted comes out clean. Be sure not to put your two loaf pans too closely together in the oven, so the heat will be distributed evenly. Let bread cool in pans 10 minutes, then turn onto a wire rack and let cool completely. Makes 2 loaves.

Spiked Carrot Bread

1¹/₂ cups	flour
¹/₂ tsp	salt
1 tsp	baking soda
¹/₄ tsp	baking powder
1 tsp	cinnamon
¹/₂ cup	vegetable oil
¹/₂ cup	brown sugar
¹/₂ cup	sugar
2	eggs
1	heaping tsp orange peel (grated)
¹/₄ cup	fresh squeezed orange juice
2 cups	shredded carrots
¹/₂ cup	chopped walnuts

Sift flour, salt, baking soda, baking powder and cinnamon into a bowl. Set aside.

Beat oil and sugars in another mixing bowl until well blended. Add eggs, orange peel and orange juice, and beat until well blended. Stir in carrots and walnuts, then flour mixture. Mix well.

Pour batter into a buttered and floured medium sized loaf pan. Bake in a 350° oven for 50-60 minutes, or until a wooden pick inserted near center comes out clean. Poke holes in bread with a toothpick and pour Orange Sauce (recipe follows) evenly over the top. Let bread cool 10 minutes in loaf pan, then turn onto a wire rack and let cool completely.

Orange Sauce

1/8 cup	Triple Sec (orange liqueur)
1/4 cup	sugar
1/8 cup	fresh squeezed orange juice
3	large pieces orange peel

Place all ingredients into a small saucepan and bring to a boil over high heat. Reduce heat to medium and continue boiling, stirring constantly for 3 minutes (or until syrup becomes frothy). Remove the orange peel pieces. Pour hot syrup directly on bread.

Banana Surprise Bread

1¾ cups	flour
1¼ tsp	baking powder
½ tsp	baking soda
¾ tsp	salt
4 tbsp	butter, softened
⅔ cup	sugar
¼ cup	vegetable oil
2	eggs
1 tsp	vanilla
2 tbsp	milk
3 tbsp	instant coconut cream pudding & pie filling
2 tsp	grated lemon peel
2	ripe bananas, mashed (medium-sized)
1 cup	angel flake coconut

-M. FALCO-

Sift together flour, baking powder, baking soda and salt. Set aside.

In a medium sized bowl with an electric mixer, beat butter and sugar until well blended. Add oil and beat until smooth and creamy. Add eggs one at a time, then the vanilla, milk, pudding mixture and lemon peel. Beat until smooth after each addition. Add flour mixture and mashed bananas alternately to creamed mixture, beating until smooth after each addition. Stir in coconut.

Pour batter into a lightly greased medium sized loaf pan. Bake in 350° oven for 60 minutes, or until a wooden pick inserted near center comes out clean. Cool in pan for 10 minutes, then turn onto a wire rack and let cool completely.

NOTE: If you wrap this bread and refrigerate overnight, the flavors have more time to blend for a better taste.

Blueberry Muffins

2 cups	flour
³/₄ cup	brown sugar
1 tbsp	double-acting baking powder
1 tsp	salt
1	egg
²/₃ cup	milk
¹/₃ cup	sour cream
4 tbsp	melted butter, cooled to room temperature
1 cup	blueberries

In a large bowl, mix flour, sugar, baking powder and salt, with a fork.

In a small bowl, slightly beat egg. Stir in milk, sour cream and melted butter. Mix well. Gently stir in blueberries.

Add egg mixture all at once to the flour mixture. Stir just until flour is moistened. (Avoid overmixing, which causes toughness. Batter should be lumpy.)

Spoon batter into greased muffin-pan. Bake 20 to 25 minutes in a 400° oven until golden, and toothpick inserted in center of muffin comes out clean. Immediately remove muffins from pan onto a wire rack; serve at once. Makes 12 muffins.

Desserts

—M. FALCO—

1 QUART

Julie's All Out Chocolate Chip Cookies

EVERYBODY OUT!

Starting a business with these cookies has been discussed more than once by everyone that has tried them. The secret is 1) not skimping, and 2) using only the purest butter, chocolate and vanilla.

½ cup	butter, softened
2	eggs
¾ cup	brown sugar
⅔ cup	white sugar
2 tsp	pure vanilla
1 tsp	salt
1 tsp	baking soda
1⅓ cups	Instant Quaker Oats
1⅓ cups	all purpose flour
12 oz	pure chocolate chips
12 oz	package walnuts, coarsely chopped
1 cup	raisins

In a large mixing bowl, add the butter, eggs, brown sugar, white sugar, vanilla, salt and baking soda. Beat with electric mixer on medium speed until smooth. Mix in oatmeal and flour, a little at a time, until thoroughly blended. With a wooden spoon, stir in the chocolate chips, walnuts and raisins. Mix well.

By the tablespoon, drop 12 spoons of dough onto an ungreased cookie sheet. Bake in a 350° oven for 8-10 minutes, or until lightly browned. Makes 3 dozen large cookies.

Chewy Chocolate Coconut Bars

If you're the type who likes to place your chocolate bars in the freezer before eating, try the same with these tasty bars.

6 tbsp	butter, softened
¼ cup	sugar
¼ tsp	salt
1½ cups	walnuts, finely ground
12 oz	package semi-sweet chocolate mini morsels
1½ cups	angel flake coconut
½ cup	walnuts, chopped
14 oz	can sweetened condensed milk

With an electric mixer, beat butter for 30 seconds. Add the sugar and salt, beating until fluffy. Add the 1½ cups finely ground walnuts, and beat until well combined.

Grease the sides of a 12x8x2 inch baking pan. Spread the mixture evenly on the bottom. Next, layer in order the chocolate, coconut and ½ cup chopped walnuts. Pour sweetened condensed milk evenly over the top.

Bake in a 350° oven for 30 minutes. Let cool for 20 minutes, then place in refrigerator for about 30 minutes or until chocolate is set. Cut into bars. Store either in the refrigerator or freezer. Makes about 24 bars.

-M.FALCO-

Esther's Leckerli Bars

An old Swiss recipe which brings back memories of Christmas as a kid! These bars make tasty Christmas gifts in attractive tins, or are great to serve any time.

5 cups	sifted flour	⅛ cup	brandy (optional)
3 tsp	cinnamon	1 cup	candied orange rind
1 tsp	cloves	1 cup	candied lemon rind
1 tsp	baking soda	2 cups	walnuts, coarsely
2 cups	honey		chopped
2 cups	brown sugar	2 cups	powdered sugar
¼ cup	butter	3 tbsp	lemon juice

In a large bowl, stir together the flour, cinnamon, cloves and baking soda.

In a large saucepan, heat honey and brown sugar until sugar is dissolved. Remove from heat, and stir in the butter.

Stir the flour mixture into the honey and sugar. Then stir in the brandy, candied rind and walnuts until well combined.

While dough is still warm, spread evenly on two baking sheets sprayed well with Pam (we have tried other shortenings and this works the best) rather thinly. Bake in a 350° oven for 30-40 minutes.

In a small bowl combine the powdered sugar and lemon juice. When you remove the cooked dough from the oven, frost immediately, and cut into bars with a sharp knife while still warm. Let cool.

Store in a tightly covered container for at least a week. Makes approximately 108 2x2 inch bars.

Peanut and Honey Squares

This is a great tasting all natural dessert, or pick-me-up bar during those often too busy days.

2 cups	puffed brown rice
1 cup	pecans, chopped
1 cup	walnuts, chopped
1 cup	raisins
1/2 cup	sesame seeds
1/2 cup	carob chips
1 cup	chunky peanut butter
3/4 cup	clover honey

In a large bowl, add puffed rice, pecans, walnuts, raisins, sesame seeds and carob chips. Mix well.

Put peanut butter and honey into a medium sized saucepan. Place over medium low heat, stirring constantly until blended and smooth. Pour over puffed rice mixture, and stir until well combined.

Firmly pat mixture evenly into a large square pan. Refrigerate 2-4 hours; cut into squares. Makes 20 yummy squares.

Tropical Cake

1	pkg Duncan Hines yellow cake mix
4	eggs
1 cup	water
1/2 cup	sweetened condensed milk
1/2 cup	softened butter
1 3 1/2 oz.	pkg. instant coconut cream pudding & pie filling

- - - - - - - - - - - - - - -

1 3 oz.	package Cook 'N Serve lemon Jell-O pudding & pie filling
1/2 cup	sugar
2	egg yolks

- - - - - - - - - - - - - - -

1 pint	whipping cream
1/4 cup	powdered sugar
1 tsp	vanilla

- - - - - - - - - - - - - - -

2	medium sized bananas
1/2 cup	angel flake coconut

Follow Duncan Hines rich recipe as follows: Blend on low speed yellow cake mix, eggs, water, condensed milk, butter and coconut pudding until moistened. Mix at medium speed for 2 minutes. Pour batter in two 9" round cake pans and bake in a 350° oven for 40-45 minutes, or until toothpick inserted near center comes out clean. Let cool in pan on rack for 15 minutes. Remove from pan onto a wire rack and let cool completely.

Make the lemon pudding following the Jell-O range top recipe as follows: Mix pudding with sugar, 1/4 cup water and egg yolks. Stir in 2 cups water. Cook and stir over medium heat until mixture comes to a full boil. Cool 5 minutes, stirring twice, then let cool completely.

Pour heavy cream in chilled bowl. With an electric mixer, beat at high speed, adding powdered sugar and vanilla a little at a time, until whipping cream is firm enough to hold a shape.

To assemble cake, cut the two cake layers in half, making a total of 4 layers. Put first layer on a plate and spread with half of the lemon pudding mixture. Then, sprinkle with $1/4$ cup coconut. Add on second layer of cake, and arrange 1 thinly-sliced banana to cover layer. Cover bananas with about $1/4$ inch of the whipped cream. For third layer, repeat as on the first. Put on the final layer and arrange the second banana slices on top. Cover the top and sides of cake with remaining whipping cream. Garnish with coconut on top.

Fresh Apple Cake

1 cup	butter, softened
1 cup	sugar
½ cup	brown sugar, firmly packed
3	eggs
1 tsp	vanilla
2¼ cups	flour
1½ tsp	baking soda
1 tsp	salt
1 tsp	cinnamon
½ tsp	nutmeg
3 cups	unpeeled apples, grated
1 cup	walnuts, chopped

In a large mixing bowl, beat butter and sugars with an electric mixer until fluffy. Add the eggs and vanilla. Beat well. Add dry ingredients, beating until well combined. Stir in the apples and walnuts.

Grease and lightly flour a 12x8x2 inch baking pan. Pour cake batter into pan, and bake in a 350° oven for 40-45 minutes, or until toothpick inserted in middle comes out clean. Let cool completely, then frost with Cream Cheese Frosting (recipe follows). Makes 12-15 servings.

Cream Cheese Frosting

8 oz	cream cheese
¼ cup	butter, softened
2 tbsp	fresh lemon juice
1 tsp	fresh grated lemon peel
1½ cups	powdered sugar
1 tsp	cinnamon

In a medium sized mixing bowl, beat cream cheese and butter with an electric mixer until well blended. Add the remaining ingredients, beating until smooth.

Chocolate Walnut Cheesecake

3 cups	finely crushed graham crackers
1¾ cups	sugar
1 cup	butter
¼ cup	heavy or whipping cream
12 oz	package pure chocolate chips
24 oz	cream cheese, softened
3	eggs
2 cups	sour cream
1 tsp	vanilla
10 oz	package chopped walnuts

In a small mixing bowl, stir together graham cracker crumbs and ½ cup of the sugar. Melt butter, and stir into graham cracker crumbs. Pat crumb mixture evenly in bottom and sides of two 9 inch pie pans.

In a medium sized saucepan, add cream and chocolate chips. Place over medium-low heat. Stir constantly, until chocolate chips have melted.

In a large mixing bowl with electric mixer, beat the chocolate mixture and all remaining ingredients except for walnuts, until smooth and creamy. Stir in the walnuts. Fill the pie crusts with cheesecake mixture. Bake about 1 hour in a 350° oven. Let them cool, then refrigerate 2-3 hours before serving. Makes 2 cheesecakes.

Queen Mother's German Chocolate Cake

This cake is only for the serious chocolate lover who is willing to spend the time and money to make this delicious, rich cake. Originally this cake was made for a large office party, so naturally we wanted to make a cake that everyone would still be talking about a week later. Days were spent going through cake recipes trying to find a rich, moist, outrageous chocolate cake and then we found Queen Mother's Cake. A German chocolate filling was added and chocolate icing to make the cake complete. The cake turned out too good to be true! Please note the ingredient list is correct. The original Queen Mother's cake recipe is made three times to make this cake (that's right, three times).

Cake:

18 oz	sweet or semisweet chocolate, coarsely cut or broken
18 oz	butter (2¼ cups)
2¼ cups	sugar
18	eggs separated (separate 6 at a time)
18 oz	(3¾ cups) almonds, finely ground (the consistency of coarse flour)
⅜ tsp	salt
¼ cup	fine dry white bread crumbs

Coconut-Pecan Frosting:

2	eggs
2	5¹/₂ oz cans (1¹/₃ cups) evaporated milk
1¹/₃ cups	sugar
¹/₂ cup	butter or margarine
¹/₈ tsp	salt
2²/₃ cups	flaked coconut
1 cup	pecans, chopped

Chocolate Icing:

4 oz	(4 squares) unsweetened chocolate
1 cup	confectioners sugar
1 tbsp	hot water
2	eggs
3 oz	(6 tbsp) butter, cut in 4 pieces

Adjust rack to one-third up from the bottom of the oven. Preheat oven to 375°. Butter a 9x2¹/₂-or 3 inch spring-form pan and line the bottom with waxed paper. Butter the paper and dust all over it lightly with fine, dry white bread crumbs.

Melt 6 oz sweet or semisweet chocolate in top of small double boiler over hot water on low heat. Remove from heat and set aside to cool slightly.

In a small bowl, cream ³/₄ cup butter. Add ³/₄ cup sugar and beat at medium high speed for 2-3 minutes. Add 6 egg yolks one at a time, beating until each addition is thoroughly mixed. Beat in the melted chocolate and then, on lowest speed, gradually beat in 1¹/₄ cups ground almonds. Transfer to a large mixing bowl.

In a large bowl, beat ¹/₈ teaspoon salt with 6 egg whites until they hold a definite shape, or are stiff but not dry. Stir a large spoonful of the whites into the chocolate and then, in three additions, fold in the balance.

Turn into pan and level the top by rotating pan briskly from side to side. Bake for 20 minutes at 375°. Reduce oven temperature to 350° and continue baking for 50 minutes. (Total baking time is 1 hour and 10 minutes.) **DO NOT OVERBAKE.** Cake should remain soft and moist in the center.

Wet and slightly wring out a folded towel and place it on a smooth surface. Remove spring form from oven and place it directly on the wet towel. Let stand 20 minutes. Remove sides of spring form. Place a rack over the cake and carefully invert. Remove bottom of form and paper lining. Cover with another rack and invert again to cool right side up. Repeat the above procedure three times.

For Coconut-Pecan Frosting, in a saucepan beat egg slightly. Stir in milk, sugar, butter and salt. Cook and stir over medium heat until thickened and bubbly. Stir in coconut and pecans. Cool thoroughly.

Start to assemble the cake, putting first layer on a cake plate. Spread with a generous amount of Coconut-Pecan Frosting. Put second layer on top of first and repeat directions. Place third layer on top. Make chocolate icing by melting chocolate in top of small double boiler over hot water on medium high heat. Transfer to small bowl and immediately beat in sugar, water and eggs. Beat at moderately high speed until smooth. Beat in butter, one piece at a time, beating smooth after each addition. Pour over top of cake. Work quickly before icing sets. With a long, narrow metal spatula, smooth icing, letting it run down the sides, then smooth the sides.

Decorate the cake with left-over frosting and chocolate curls. Cover cake and refrigerate overnight.

Index

❤

♥

♥

♥

NOTES

NOTES

NOTES

NOTES

About the Chefs

Julie Lilly

Julie Lilly was born and raised in Oregon, and moved to Southern California in 1979. She married William Belote in 1986 and together they own Julie Lilly Photography, Music House Productions and Lilly & Belote Publishing. Her first screenplay, entitled, "Lost in Hollywood", is based on the true story of finding her real father (Hollywood Actor Ross Hagen), and was completed in April of 1989.

Tracy Montero

Tracy Montero was born and raised in California, and moved to Oregon in 1972. She married Lanny Montero in 1986 and together they set up home in Beaverton, Oregon, along with their children from previous marriages. Among her many talents are cooking, creative quilt making, gardening and home decorating.

❤

About the Artist

Mike Falco
Primitive Artist

Mike Falco, one of America's foremost primitive artists, was born in Brooklyn, New York, where his early years were spent on a farm.

His paintings are in the collections of many of the most sophisticated patrons of the arts throughout the United States, as well as in many museums and university collections.

Although he was successful in office work on the East Coast, Mike felt restless and made the trek westward to California to find whatever it was that caused the wandering urge within him. Through help of Hollywood friends, Mike became active in the performing arts, working as an actor in many television shows and commercials, yet this, too, failed to sum up his endless pursuit for a life's working career.

It wasn't until he was in his thirties that Mike discovered he had an enormous talent for fine art, and in less than one year, his paintings were in the collection of two Museums. Thus began the growth of one of America's most respected and distinguished primitive artists.

His work is filled with warmth, humor and charm that delights all viewers who understand the impact of skilled untrained artists. Many compare him to the small handful primitive greats such as Moses, Russo, Blair and others who share this wonderful gift that he has. Still, Mike feels he is only a channel from a higher source when he picks up his brush to start a new piece of work.

Whatever it is or wherever his talent comes from, we benefit from that unique gift and delight in his illustrations.